CHANGING IDENTITIES

CHANGING IDENTITIES

Reading and Writing Ourselves

edited by Stan Fogel
and Lynette Thoman

Canadian Scholars' Press Inc. / Toronto

Changing Identities: Reading and Writing Ourselves
Edited by Stan Fogel and Lynette Thoman

First published in 2002 by
Canadian Scholars' Press Inc.
180 Bloor Street West, Suite 1202
Toronto, Ontario
M5S 2V6

www.cspi.org

Copyright © 2002 Stan Fogel, Lynette Thoman, and Canadian Scholars' Press Inc. All rights reserved. No part of this publication may be photocopied, reproduced, stored in a retrieval system, or transmitted, in any form or by any means, electronic, mechanical or otherwise, without the written permission of Canadian Scholars' Press Inc., except for brief passages quoted for review purposes. In the case of photocopying, a licence from CANCOPY may be obtained.

Every reasonable effort has been made to identify copyright holders. CSPI would be pleased to have any errors or omissions brought to its attention.

CSPI gratefully acknowledges the financial support of the Government of Canada through the Book Publishing Industry Development Program for our publishing activities.

National Library of Canada Cataloguing in Publication Data

Main entry under title:

    Changing identities : reading and writing ourselves / edited by Stan Fogel and Lynette Thoman.

ISBN 1-55130-216-0

1. Canadian essays (English)—20th century. 2. College readers.
I. Fogel, Stanley II. Thoman, Lynette, 1969–

PS8373.C44 2002   C814'.5408   C2002-903048-X
PR9197.7.C44 2002

Page design and layout by Susan Thomas/Digital Zone
Cover design by George Kirkpatrick

02   03   04   05   06   07   7   6   5   4   3   2   1

Printed and bound in Canada by AGMV Marquis

Acknowledgements

Abdel-Shehid, Gamal. "Raptor Morality: Blacks, Basketball and National Identity." *Borderlines*, No. 45. Reprinted by permission of the author.

Adams, Mary Louise. "So what's wrong with *wussy* sports?" *Borderlines*, No. 46. Reprinted by permission of the author.

augustine, karen/miranda. "bizarre women, exotic bodies & outrageous sex: or if annie sprinkle was a black ho she wouldn't be all that." *Borderlines*, No. 32. Reprinted by permission of the author.

Bayoumi, Moustafa. "MY Passport, MY Self." *Borderlines*, No. 40. Reprinted by permission of the author.

Butala, Sharon. "Telling the Truth." Published in *Brick*, No. 49, and in *Prairie Schooner* 67:4 (Winter 1993). Reprinted by permission of the author.

Choy, Wayson. Excerpt from *Paper Shadows* by Wayson Choy. Copyright © 1999 by Wayson Choy. Reprinted by permission of Penguin Books Canada Limited.

Connelly, Karen. Excerpt from *Touch the Dragon: A Thai Journal* by Karen Connelly. Copyright © 1992 Karen Connelly. Reprinted by permission of Turnstone Press.

Delany, Sheila. "My Mother's Feet" from *Telling Hours: Journal Stories* by Sheila Delany. Vancouver: New Star Books, 1991. Reprinted by permission of the author.

Dragu, Margaret and A.S.A. Harrison. Excerpt from *Revelations: Essays on Striptease and Sexuality* by Margaret Dragu and A.S.A. Harrison. London, On.: Nightwood Editions, 1988. Reprinted by permission of the publisher.

Fawcett, Brian. Excerpts from *Gender Wars: A Novel and Some Conversation about Sex and Gender*. Toronto: Somerville House, 1994. Reprinted by permission of the author.

Fogel, Stan. "The Marshalls: No Island Is an Island" from *Gringo Star* by Stan Fogel. Toronto: ECW Press, 1995. Reprinted by permission of the publisher.

Gallant, Mavis. Introduction to *The Selected Stories of Mavis Gallant*, by Mavis Gallant. Copyright © 1996 by Mavis Gallant. Reprinted by permission of Georges Borchardt, Inc., Literary Agency.

Gandesha, Samir. "New York City Man." *Borderlines*, No. 47. Reprinted by permission of the author.

Huston, Nancy. "Dealing With What's Dealt." *Brick*, No. 52. Reprinted by permission of the author. All rights reserved by the author.

Kates, Joanne. "For the Love of the Cheese," from *The Taste of Things* by Joanne Kates. Toronto: Oxford University Press, 1987. Reprinted by permission of the author.

Khan, Shahnaz. "The Space Beneath My Feet." Preface from *Aversion and Desire: Negotiating Muslim Female Identity in the Diaspora* by Shahnaz Khan. Toronto: Women's Press, 2002. Reprinted by permission of the publisher.

McCormack, Eric. "Less Than Meets the Eye." *New Quarterly*, Fall 1993. Reprinted by permission of the author.

Millard, Laura. "Images of Canada: Canadian Bank Notes." *Borderlines*, No. 28. Reprinted by permission of the publisher.

Nadel, Ira. Excerpt from *Leonard Cohen: A Life in Art* by Ira Nadel. Toronto: ECW Press, 1994. Reprinted by permission of the publisher.

Persky, Stan. Excerpt from *Autobiography of a Tattoo*. Vancouver: New Star Books, 1997. Reprinted by permission of the publisher.

Pevere, Geoff, and Greig Dymond. Excerpts from *Mondo Canuck: An Encyclopedia of Canadian Pop Culture* by Geoff Pevere and Greig Dymond. Copyright © 1996 by Geoff Pevere and Greig Dymond. Reprinted by permission of Penguin Books Canada Limited.

Richler, Daniel. "Books on T.V.," from *One on One*. Ed. L. Crouch. Toronto: Somerville House, 1994. Reprinted by permission of the author.

Roberts, Paul William. Excerpt from *River in the Desert: Modern Travels in Ancient Egypt*. Toronto: Random House, 1993. Reprinted by permission of the author.

Rybczynski, Witold. "Comfort and Well Being," pp. 217–32, from *Home: A Short History of an Idea* by Witold Rybczynski. Copyright © 1986 by Witold Rybczynski. Used by permission of Viking Penguin, a division of Penguin Putnam Inc.

Table of Contents

Introduction 1

Gender 5
Introduction 5
   1. Sheila Delany, "My Mother's Feet" 5
   2. Nancy Huston, "Dealing with What's Dealt" 12
   3. Brian Fawcett, excerpts, *Gender Wars* 27

Race 35
Introduction 35
   1. Shahnaz Khan, "The Space Beneath My Feet" 35
   2. Moustafa Bayoumi, "MY Passport, MY Self" 46
   3. Wayson Choy, excerpt, *Paper Shadows* 52

Sexuality 63
Introduction 63
   1. Stan Persky, excerpt, *Autobiography of a Tattoo* 63
   2. Margaret Dragu and A.S.A. Harrison, excerpt, *Revelations: Essays on Striptease and Sexuality* 71
   3. karen/miranda augustine, "bizarre women, exotic bodies & outrageous sex..." 81

Media 87
Introduction 87
   1. Daniel Richler, "Books on T.V." 88

2. Ira Nadel, excerpt, *Leonard Cohen: A Life in Art* 92
  3. Samir Gandesha, "New York City Man" 100

Style 107
Introduction 107
  1. Joanne Kates, "For the Love of the Cheese" 107
  2. Witold Rybczynski, excerpt, *Home: A Short History of an Idea* 112
  3. Laura Millard, "Images of Canada: Canadian Bank Notes" 120

Sports 131
Introduction 131
  1. Gamal Abdel-Shehid, "Raptor Morality: Blacks, Basketball and National Identity" 131
  2. Mary Louise Adams, "So what's wrong with *wussy* sports?" 138
  3. Geoff Pevere and Greig Dymond, excerpts, *Mondo Canuck: An Encyclopedia of Canadian Pop Culture* 146

Travel 151
Introduction 151
  1. Paul William Roberts, excerpt, *River in the Desert* 151
  2. Stan Fogel, "The Marshalls: No Island Is an Island" 160
  3. Karen Connelly, excerpt, *Touch the Dragon: A Thai Journal* 166

Literature 177
Introduction 177
  1. Eric McCormack, "Less than Meets the Eye" 177
  2. Mavis Gallant, Introduction from *The Selected Stories of Mavis Gallant* 188
  3. Sharon Butala, "Telling the Truth" 201

Glossary of Useful Terms 209

CHANGING IDENTITIES

Introduction

WHEN I WAS LEARNING HOW to play tennis—long enough ago that all rackets were made of wood—the rule was: stand sideways to the net and swing your racket in a semi-circle parallel to the ground. Then along came a Swede with long hair and a headband. (Those were the "hippie" days, remember; clothing styles as well as life styles were changing.) His name was Bjorn Borg and he rose through the ranks of tennis professionals to become number one in the world. He achieved that ranking by breaking the rule I cited above. He hit the ball facing the net; dropping his racket to ankle-level, he then whipped it up, above his shoulders, imparting top-spin to the ball. Now, of course, almost every great player hits the ball that way.

Where is the significance to essay writing in all of this, you may ask. Well, when I was producing essays—about the same time I was hitting tennis balls without top-spin, the rule one was never permitted to violate was: avoid using the word "I" in an academic paper. Who was I (or who were you), so went the argument, to use "I"? It was considered presumptuous for a student to identify him or herself; it was also regarded as far too impressionistic. It would have given legitimacy to anyone's point-of-view, even—gasp!—a student's.

Have you examined many academic essays lately? Probably not, so let me tell you that "I"s are everywhere. A famous cultural and literary critic, Gayatri Chakravorty Spivak, has not only often introduced herself as "I," but she has also revealed "upfront" her specific political perspective. Look, too, at the following sentences from a scholarly essay called "Teledildonics": "How to make sense of bodies? Lesbians are asked to account for our bodies...by the dominant culture...." That frank admission regarding "our" bodies, which includes the writer in the group she is studying, is again a radical departure from what once was a reputedly uninvolved authorial norm.

Here is one final example: Lee Quinby, in a book called *Anti-Apocalypse*, begins an essay on the Black American writer Zora Neale Hurston by reminiscing that she, Quinby, grew up in the same city as Hurston; however, not only had she not heard of Hurston, she had never even been to the part of town in which Hurston had lived. This personal anecdote allows Quinby to explore issues of race, society and culture that previously were only presented by critics, if they were raised at all, in the context of Hurston's books. That Quinby is white and Hurston was black is, for the former, important to her study of Hurston's works.

So, some things have changed, in essay writing as in tennis. Introducing tennis as I did, though, drawing a comparison between two seemingly unrelated things, is a time-tested tactic of writing. Some things, it is clear, have not changed. Nonetheless, the model for essay writing has been altered significantly and it is for that reason Lynette Thoman and I have put together this reader.

Most notably, many of us now write from a self-identified position. Instead of only being writers—or, for that matter, readers—we now sign ourselves as, for example, male or female—or transgendered—writers. We often write, if we are people of colour, with that in mind. We acknowledge—in print—our gayness or straightness or bi-sexuality. We divulge our political point-of-view on the spectrum of left to right.

Furthermore, it is important to draw your attention to the fact that all the models we have chosen are drawn from Canadian sources. Most, in addition, are from what is called the "alternative" press; that is, so-called "small" magazines and presses, many of them publicly funded. These editorial decisions clearly shape what you will read in the following pages.

Many of the pieces herein you might find provocative. This, too, was our choice. None of the selections is given to you as an ideal—a perfect model. We don't believe there is such a thing, no matter how many famous essays—by George Orwell, say, or E.M. Forster, mid-twentieth century British writers—are usually offered up as models. All essays incorporate various strategies; their authors convince some people, but not others, by means of their tactics. Any essay, we think, provides the opportunity for acceptance or resistance—a space for your reaction.

When your reaction takes the form of an essay, it will be equally vulnerable, open to appreciation and to criticism. Introducing a grammar book she has published, Karen Elizabeth Gordon writes, "If you nuzzle these pages with abandon, writing will lose its terror and your sentences their disarray." We can't promise, perhaps, that the essays that follow will work as magically as Gordon thinks her instructional manual will. (She is optimistically holding out hope that a love of the intricacies of language will improve your prose.) We do, however, think that a committed reading of these essays—their content and the ways they work—will stimulate you to produce your own written response…with a heightened awareness of how best to present your argument.

*   *   *   *

Gender, race, sexuality, media, style, sports, travel, literature: we have chosen these categories because to a greater or lesser degree they impinge on all of our lives much of the time. They are not meant to be exclusive, nor are the articles chosen to represent these headings meant to cover all aspects of the subject. The first three, of course, influence greatly how we respond to the world around us—and to ourselves. The others, though, can be major preoccupations for us and can shape who we are and what we think.

—Stan Fogel

Gender

SINCE THE MID-SIXTIES, when Betty Friedan, Germaine Greer and Gloria Steinem wrote ground-breaking texts that put into question traditional female practices, there has been a veritable explosion of texts that re-examine what "masculine" and "feminine" mean. That outpouring of feminist insights has continued unabated; it has also produced a reaction from some women (notably Camille Paglia) as well as divisions over such issues as, say, pornography. On the one hand, Susie Bright, in her series called *Herotica, Erotic Fiction By Women*, champions a liberated sexuality; on the other hand, Catherine Mackinnon and Andrea Dworkin resist women's incursion into pornographic realms. Regardless, women have increasingly redefined the ways our genders are understood. This has forced men, too, to scrutinize their notions of male and female. Even the more frequent use of the word "gender" indicates a shift in our comprehension of this aspect of ourselves.

SHEILA DELANY,

"My Mother's Feet"

Body imaging is, of course, an especially impactful issue for women. Anorexia and bulimia have often been chronicled as social diseases; advertisers and couturiers have been censured for presenting impossibly slim women as ideals. Here, in the following story, Sheila Delany celebrates her mother's femininity in terms of the latter's…feet! The entire portrait is tenderly presented and extended into the sweet consideration of a mother-daughter relationship. Intimacy, sexuality, frankness: all these elements are present in Delany's homage to her mother.

Questions:

1. Delany writes that her mother "alienated her own body to the current ideal of femininity." How does Delany produce the portrait of her mother as a heavy, lovely woman?
2. What is the traditional woman vs. (post)modern woman opposition Delany plays on in her piece?
3. Do you think that the shift in focus from the mother's feet to the narrator's birth-control needs succeeds? Why?
4. Highlighting her mother's feet gives Delany's essay an original, unclichéd feel. Do you agree with this statement?
5. "Journal Stories": this is the subtitle for the collection from which the story is taken. Discuss this label—is it a contradictory designation?

This memoir is written "in white ink," as Hélène Cixous calls it: that which remains in us of the mother "as nonname and as source of goods," the one who in giving her body as text gives us our own body and therefore, in less tangible ways, our texts. The story describes two moments of discovery and assertion—with my mother and against her—that occurred when I was four and seventeen, or perhaps three and seventeen; they are always linked, in my mind, by the importance of my mother's feet.

I never saw my mother's body. I saw her naked, of course, as we were not a puritanical family. But the body that existed for me was not the one that had existed before me: so testified photographs of my mother as a young woman. There, in the brown-tinted photos, she was slender and small-boned, cameo-faced and dreamy-eyed—though with a stubborn set to the jaw that bespoke struggles I would learn of years later: to keep part of the salary from her first job rather than turn it over to her father; to retrieve her mother from a state mental hospital after my grandmother's nervous breakdown; to organize unions in New England factories during the late thirties; to give birth to me while my father, a musician, was on tour with the band he worked for. (He was in Georgia at the time, where there were autumn hurricanes. The birth, a difficult one, was the first for the young doctor in attendance, who subsequently left obstetrics for a less harrowing career in general practice. It was 1940.)

The body I came to know was not that of the slim, stubborn beauty in the brown photographs, for after giving birth to me and my sister in a year and a half, my mother put on weight. She was what, in the forties, used to be called "pleasingly plump." It was an era when curves were in style, and a little more flesh never hurt. "A lot of woman," "more of you to love," "woman's glory," "better too much than too little"—these are the phrases that come to mind. My mother remained attractive even with the extra weight, for she had fine warm skin, expressive eyes, and dark, waving hair that she was excessively proud of. She wore her hair very long—usually braided around her head or, for special occasions, in a chignon. Washing her hair was a ceremony, and it took hours to dry, spread out and flowing down her back. Nonetheless my mother grew heavier with the years and through most of my childhood she was obese. To this day a normal physique appears "scrawny" in her eyes, an offense against nature which it is her duty to transform into a reassuringly rounded object through the assiduous administration of food. "Fatten up!" she remonstrates, half-joking, over the phone the day after we have lunched together. In short, the body I knew was not my mother's real body but a bloated and venous imitation of her real body, bellied and large-breasted, small hands emerging from fat-cuffed forearms, fine-boned face collared in jowl.

The old photographs show that my mother was not, in her early twenties, a large-bosomed woman. That she became so was a transformation gratifying to my father in more ways than one, for he took credit for the "improvement" of her figure. Marriage and pregnancy caused her to bloom, he claimed. "You were flat-chested when I married you!" he would exult, her avoirdupois the living sign of his efficacy. For both of them, in fact, it was not simply unattractive but nearly offensive for a woman to be thin or small-breasted, so that it was with a certain smugness that the two of them might privately criticize or mock some acquaintance or celebrity: "Skinny marintz! Nothing to hold on to! All that meat and no potatoes!" My mother alienated her own body to the current ideal of femininity; it is now some forty years since she has had her own body.

Certainly the importance of my mother's overweight—its representative or symbolic value—can't have been only an accommodation to a particular conception of female beauty. Indeed it soon transcended that and became its opposite: a display of disdain for the triviality of having to appear conventionally attractive. As a mother, one no longer had to deprive oneself of the pleasure of food, to discipline oneself that way, for one had one's man and had proved one's social value in being a mother. "You see?" it says, "I can afford to indulge myself." "Afford" psychologically, for upward social mobility surely reinforced the accumulative impulse, given the immigrant poverty from which both parents sprang. It seems that maternity and mobility worked together to produce a solid citizen and person of substance, one with the desire to *embody* her significance, her meaning, her power.

What power? Very simply, a mother's over her child. That was the power I withdrew from when, at three or four, I denied the bloated body that represented it, in a scene that remains perfectly clear in my memory. My mother and I are talking about this and that. I inquire how babies are fed. "From their mother's breast," she replies, and, lifting the naked breast out of her blouse, "Want to try?" It was with indignant revulsion that I turned down the offer. In part this was an aesthetic refusal of the object itself: full but flaccid, blue-veined, and pale with its disk of brown areola. How could one even grapple with it, come to terms with it? I was

GENDER

refusing, too, the dependent-submissive role of a nursing child, a role once and for all outgrown. I know I saw the breast as a means of domination, and interpreted my mother's offer in the worst Machiavellian light.

(Now, after having nursed two children, I am inclined to be more charitable. What does my mother's gesture reveal about her? That she was not prudish, certainly. That she looked back at the period of nursing with love, and missed it. That she valued her body for what it had been able to give, and to be, to her children. Most likely she was extending a wish for continued nurturance and protection—a maternal blessing, whose best fulfilment is to be passed on again. So, at least, I am able to receive it now—though still without regret for my instinctive refusal, which was necessary at the time.)

There was, though, a part of my mother's body that I did like, and it was her feet: specifically the soles of her feet, which were covered with a thick layer of translucent yellowish callus. I aspired to such feet, admired and envied them, much to my mother's puzzled disgust at this aberration. Despite the disfiguring shield of fat in which her body was losing itself, my mother's lower legs retained a firm shapeliness, and her strong feet with their hardened soles seemed to represent the absent living body, like the hank of real hair on a voodoo doll. That layer of yellowish callus seemed the only thing about her that was genuinely tough and natural. It referred to unconventional behaviour—going barefoot, feeling the floor directly—of a sort that she rarely acknowledged. It revealed something about her that I wished were more overt, more continuously present: a lost inner self that I hoped was recoverable—if not in her, then perhaps some day in myself. It signified an intuitive quality that I generally missed in her relations with me and my sister. It was her real body, unmediated, there where it met the world and showed the results of such an encounter, beyond makeup or manipulation: no sign of control but rather of interaction with, implicitly, everything out there beyond the walls of our little apartment, out there in the enormous city where I yearned to go. So that my mother's calloused feet constituted no imperfection in my eyes, but were the part of her body that I wholeheartedly admired.

The second time that my mother's feet became important was some thirteen or fourteen years later. We had moved in the meantime, and now lived in a suburban house in southern New England. My father still played music, but he had also made a successful career in insurance and estate planning. It was just before my departure for college, and conversations with my mother tended to include a good deal of advice from her on living in general. Again the scene is vivid in my mind. I have just emerged from the bath, and am anointing myself with a pink lotion, faintly spice-smelling.

"Don't forget your feet," Mother advises, "so that when you are my age you will be complimented on your femininity—as I," she continues with dignity, "have been complimented on mine." She shows me all the little neglected and potentially rough spots that will benefit from the frequent application of lotion: ankles, toe knuckles, back of heels.

The compliment, it turned out, had come from a friend of my parents: a handsome, cultivated man somewhat older than themselves, a short, dark, pipe-smoking and tidily bearded European—he was Danish, I believe—who taught at a small local college. Lars Gunderson was married, and the two couples had met at some cultural event or other, a lecture or concert in town. In front of me and my sister, my mother always referred to Lars as "Doctor Gunderson" out of respect for his advanced degree. Between him and my mother there existed a certain semi-flirtatious bond, though neither of them, I am sure, would seriously have entertained the idea of an affair. They seemed rather to share a sense of what they might have been to one another had they been unattached. Nonetheless, my father enjoyed playing the part of a slightly jealous husband: he would twit my mother on her "crush" or her "admirer" and take every opportunity to parody Lars's somewhat pompous old-style European manner.

It was in another of these pre-departure conversations that my mother made what struck me as a magnanimous offer:

"If—when—you feel you need birth-control information, don't hesitate to ask me." Having worked as a nurse before marriage, and later as a social worker, my mother was making an effort to be objective, professional: she had seen enough of adolescent pregnancies and illicit abortions. How proud I was of such enlightenment! I took the promise away with me like the talisman bestowed by a good fairy at journey's start: at once magical protection and open sesame to real life.

Not many months later I wrote home to have the offer made good. An agitated telephone call was the response, requiring my return that very weekend. It had been arranged, I found, for me to discuss the weighty matter with no less an authority than my parents' professor friend Dr. Gunderson. So there we were in an old-fashioned study: walls of books, heavy dark desk with green-shaded lamp, and the doctor himself thoughtfully puffing his pipe as he sat relaxed in a leather armchair. He was pleasant enough; he was liberal and tactful. He reminisced about his own days in college, lamenting the wonderful papers he had written in those days. "They were so incisive," he said, "I could never write anything so incisive now." There was no interrogation that I can recall, no denunciation, and certainly no information. There was only reiterated concern for the guilt the good doctor claimed I would inevitably feel later on.

I returned to my country campus. I wrote to my best friend who was living in New York, saying that I would spend Christmas vacation with her. I asked her to make an appointment for me at the Margaret Sanger Clinic so that I could get a diaphragm.

The day came. Jane and I devised my cover story, the story that must prove the legitimacy of my presence at the clinic. I was engaged (I invented names and addresses), we could not marry because we were both in school, our parents opposed the match for religious reasons, my rabbi in Boston had referred me to the clinic and would be happy to write a letter if one were required. Irresistible, we thought. I went in alone, as befitted a star-crossed young fiancée. There was an interview, an examination and fitting, and then the precious prescription was in my hands. "We believe your story," said the woman doctor who handed it over, "because you were so relaxed during the examination. If it weren't true you'd have been tense. Good luck." A stop at the nearest drugstore, where it seemed hundreds of the wonderful inventions were stacked in neat little boxes, a tube of spermicidal jelly, then home to Jane's to celebrate our success.

Did I tell my mother that I'd managed without her information? I don't think so. Probably not, because I felt so deeply betrayed by her change of mind, her transformation from liberated and liberating good fairy back into the conventional controlling mother I'd always resisted. And what faith she had in Lars—a man who couldn't even write an incisive paper any more! The puzzle is, though, why she thought—or whether she thought—that her refusal would have any effect. It was almost as if, in her idea of it, we inhabited a fairy-tale world, without magazine articles, without television documentaries, without books, and as if she were really custodian of the magic word.

Funnily enough, I am now about the age my mother was when these events occurred, and, as it happens, I am regularly complimented on my femininity by a handsome and rather old-fashioned friend, also a professor, also married. It amuses me that this bit of personal history should repeat itself, exactly as it was meant to do. Appreciating that repetition, I see my independence not only against my mother but because of her. If I resisted her successfully, if I fought off her domination effectively—if I was relaxed on the Sanger clinic's examination table—I was enabled to do it in part by her gifts: some of them deliberate and acknowledged, others cleverly concealed but still as traceable as that translucent yellow callus that covered her feet.

NANCY HUSTON,

"Dealing with What's Dealt"

This is a dazzling essay, startling in its introduction and provocative in its innards. From the boldness of the "I'm beautiful," its first sentence, to its contention that the author benefitted from trysts/relations with teachers (older, male), Nancy Huston writes fearlessly and frankly about herself—as well as about some controversial issues. She is unrepentant about her amours and insistent that desire plays an important role in the classroom. She resists not only the sanitization of the student body; she also contests the North American fetish for banning "unwholesome" practices such as smoking or staring at and flirting with those to whom one is attracted. Reading and rereading "Dealing with What's Dealt" made me want to read Huston's fiction. It will probably have the same effect on you.

Questions:

1. How does the "cards" motif get used in "Dealing with What's Dealt?"
2. Note the frequency with which Huston uses "I." What have you been told about the intrusion of yourself into the essay?
3. Can you contribute to the so-called "political correctness" debate?
4. Could someone who is not a significant writer get away with some of the statements Huston makes? Do you dare write this frankly?
5. Note the early frequency of very short sentences. How do they contribute to the overall effect of the essay?

I'm beautiful. I've never written about this before, so I thought I'd try to write about it. It's lasted quite a long time, this beauty of mine, but it won't be lasting much longer because I'm forty now, as I'm writing this, forty now and probably by the time you read it forty-one, and so on and so forth, and we all know it ends up as worms or ashes, but for the time being I'm still beautiful. More or less. Less than I used to be, despite the regular application of henna to my graying hair and concealer to the rings beneath my eyes. Less than Benazir Bhutto of Pakistan, who is precisely my age, less than many of my students now—but still, perhaps, a little more than my eleven-year-old daughter. For another year or two ("Mirror, mirror...").

I'm also intelligent. Less so than Simone Weil. My intelligence, too, is already going downhill—though differently from my beauty—and it, too, will end up as worms or ashes. But still. For the time being I'm quite intelligent.

When I say I'm beautiful and intelligent, I'm not boasting. All I've done is take reasonable care of the beauty and intelligence programmed into me by the dice-toss of my parents' chromosomes. (They were both beautiful and intelligent, too, when they were young; they're considerably less so now, but that probably doesn't interest you as much as the rest of what I have to say.) How is it possible to boast about things for which one is not responsible?

We are dealt a hand at birth: some of the cards are genetic (skin colour, musicality, bunions), others are cultural (religion, language, nationality), but all are given rather than chosen. Later, as adults, we can make a conscious decision to change a few of the cards in our hands—by converting from Catholicism to Judaism, for example, or by moving to another country, or even by having a sex-change operation—but the original deal inevitably leaves its deep and indelible imprint on us.

I've never quite understood people's boasting about their destiny-dealt hand, though it's certainly a ubiquitous phenomenon. Perhaps my own origins are too bland to have instilled in me this sort of pride: it's never occurred to me to derive self-esteem from the fact that I was born in Calgary, Alberta, or that I was raised a Protestant or that I have white skin or that I am female. Likewise, I'm responsible for neither my beauty nor my intelligence, which have been two incredibly salient features of the forty years I've spent on this earth so far—and which, until today, I've never had the courage to write about.

My beauty has gotten me many places, to some of which I very badly wanted to go, and to some of which I did not want to go at all. Over the years, I've watched it attack and corrode borders, then take me with it into foreign territories. Borders are ideas erected between age groups, social classes, all sorts of hierarchical entities, in order that society may function as predictably and as decently as possible. They are not solid brick walls. Beauty eats them away. This is the truth; we've all seen it happen, though it happens differently in different places (I'll be coming back to this).

I was not particularly beautiful as a child. I started getting that way at around age fifteen, when I was a junior in high school (I'd skipped a grade—much earlier, because my intelligence was manifest long before my beauty), and as soon as it happened I seduced and/or was seduced by my creative writing teacher. He was ten years older than I (though younger than the man to whom I'm now married), and, shortly before the end of the school year, he took whatever virginity childhood sex games with my brother had left me. I was thrilled, flattered, crazily in love, and, for a long time, proud—yes, proud, for this was something in which my responsibility was implicated. The love affair was a serious one. It culminated in engagement—an engagement I broke off at age eighteen, when I fell in love with someone else. For nearly three years, then, my life revolved around this man. There was no sexual harassment involved.

Ah, but was he not taking advantage of his position? Of his superior education? Of the intellectual awe in which I held him? He certainly was, just as I was taking advantage of my youth, beauty, and whatever innocence I still appeared to possess. We wanted the same thing, which was to be in love with each other. Were we equals? Were Socrates and the young men whom he instructed and sodomized equals? American society, it seems, would in all likelihood condemn Socrates to death just as Athens did, though for different reasons.

Let us be careful. Let us be subtle. Let us not be polemical and deliciously angry and righteously indignant. The subject is a messy one, as messy and contradictory as the species to which we belong, so let us not pretend to tie up all its loose ends and get it straight and iron it flat. Would I like the idea of my daughter sleeping with one of her teachers? No, not at age eleven. At what age, then? At an age when she has acquired a will of her own, a desire of her own, and an intellect capable of critical discernment. In other words, at an age when (and *if*, for not all young girls have the same weird penchant for brainy older men as I) she wants it. I tend to think that in her case that might mean something like never, but naturally I don't know.

Listen. Last spring I was at a literary cocktail party in Montreal, standing in a corner drinking wine with my brother and an eminent elderly Quebecois writer, and the conversation came around to the cases, currently hitting the headlines, of young boys who'd been sexually abused by priests in Quebec's Catholic schools. "The problem with this whole outcry," my brother said suddenly, "is that it'll make it impossible for actual love affairs ever to take place in those situations again." I saw the older man do a double take and then—to my utter astonishment—heard him say. "Yes, you're right. I had that experience myself. Of course, I wasn't ten or eleven years old, I was sixteen. But still...."

The man was now in his seventies. It had probably been several decades since he'd dared allude to this experience, his teen-age love for one of his teachers, but the memory of it was still vivid enough to make his voice tremble with emotion. Clearly, he had loved that teacher, just as I had loved the one to whom I later became engaged. And because we loved them, we also learned a great deal from these seductive teachers. They fed our intelligence, brought our bodies and our minds to life. I read a thousand books because of mine. Again, the child's age makes an important difference—and also his or her psychological vulnerability. I am by no means challenging the fact that students have been, can be, are being sexually manipulated or abused by their teachers. I'm only asking that we not leap from this fact to the grotesque conclusion that bodiliness should be radically eliminated from all pedagogical situations. In my own teaching experience over the years, though it so happens I've never flirted with students let alone slept with them, I'm fairly sure my beauty has contributed positively to the transmission of knowledge and ideas, the stimulation of their brains.

Other borders eaten away by my beauty I would definitely have rather seen preserved. For example, I could have done without having my thighs stroked by the grey-haired doctor who performed my first gynecological examination, or my eyes longingly stared into by the bespectacled young dentist who removed my impacted wisdom teeth. Probably since the Stone Age, beautiful (and less beautiful) girls have needed to learn to defend themselves— whether through sarcasm, cool rejection or karate chops—against these annoying infringements on their integrity. They can come from almost anyone—including, unexceptionally, women. Again, the only criterion for whether this behaviour is oppressive or not is whether or not one is made uncomfortable by it—that is, whether or not there is space and desire for response, interaction.

Still other experiences with borders strike me, so to speak, as borderline. After I finished high school and before I entered college (indeed, in order to earn money to attend college, because the gifts and advantages bestowed on me at birth had not included wealth), I worked full-time as a medical secretary in the psychiatric clinic of an august educational institution. By this time, I was seventeen and really quite beautiful, in my WASPish sort of way. I was also extraordinarily depressed. My depression may indeed have contributed to my beauty (as Bob Dylan pointed out, there is something irresistible about sad-eyed ladies). I was depressed partly because my fiancé was far away, partly because typing psychiatric records was one hell of a lousy initiation into adulthood, and partly because my superior intelligence made it painful and humiliating for me to be working full-time as a secretary. After a few months I was so suicidal that I myself entered therapy with one of my bosses. This is not a joke. The therapy was free, part of my health benefits as an employee of the august institution. The shrink whom I chose to see—regularly, alone, in his office, once or twice a week—was, naturally, the one I had come to like and respect the most, after months of transcribing his Dictaphone summaries of sessions with his patients. Indeed we had become rather chummy. He was forty, as I am now, and, like myself, not badly endowed in body and in mind—and I, as I have said, was seventeen. By the time I began lying down on his couch, I had already sat for his children a couple of times, attended some of his lectures at the august institution, and received from him as a Christmas present a wonderful pair of running-shoes (like millions of other Americans then and now, he jogged to work off his calories and his anger).

I entered therapy with him, and more borders were eaten away. No, he did not rape or maul me; he did not even crush me on the couch with the frightening weight of his body. As a matter of fact, his was a small and unprepossessing body; there was nothing frightening about it whatsoever. He kissed me, standing up, at the end of every session. I kissed him back. We mostly kissed on the lips. Sometimes on the cheeks or the neck. No tongue work, as I recall. Never the least constraint. I found the kisses comforting, and flattering, though not arousing. Perhaps he was aroused—but if he was, he never pressed it upon me. That border, at least, was preserved.

Was this a traumatizing experience? In my case, I think not. It seems to me that other acts performed by irresponsible or immature authority figures have left far deeper scars on my psyche. My first-grade teacher, for instance, who—before I skipped into second grade—slashed her red pen across my imperfect copy-book so hard that the page was torn. I'd rather be kissed than slashed any day.

Still, the question is, why did this shrink feel compelled to kiss me? As I saw it (fairly lucidly) at the time, it was partly because of my beauty and intelligence, and partly because the state of extreme fragility I was in had stimulated his protective male instincts. I say this with no irony whatsoever. In fact, I know it to be the truth because I had dinner last month with this man. I'd returned to teach for a semester at the same old august institution, we hadn't seen each other in twenty-three years, he is now nearing retirement, we still got along famously, and in the course of this dinner he told me that in 1971, when I was his patient and his secretary and his babysitter and his friend, he had longed to cast an invisible mantle of protection over my shoulders as I went out into the world.

And I believed him.

Also in the course of our dinner, he complimented me on having pulled through so well. I could see him casting about for laudative adjectives to describe me, body and soul, and for intensifying adverbs to describe the adjectives. The compliments he came up with were perfectly delightful, but it was hard for me to relish them to the full, as they were almost invariably prefaced by the demurral, "I hope you won't think I'm being patronizing." "Oh, no!" I encouraged him, in my very wannest voice. "More, more!" But deep down I was dismayed. What has been going on in this country? I wondered. Can it really have grown as dangerous as that to tell a woman she is beautiful and intelligent?

But I've gotten much too far ahead of my story.

After a year of working as a secretary, I had set aside enough money to be able to attend college, with the help of a scholarship and a loan. It was an excellent college—thanks, presumably, this time, not to my superior beauty but to my superior intelligence. By now I was eighteen and—due to the free-love ambiance in which all of us were floating in those post-Pill, pre-AIDS years—no longer innocent at all. I had slept with a frightening number of men (men could no longer frighten me—only their number). I was living with the one for whom I'd left my creative writing-teacher-fiancé. And I had decided to study, among other things, creative writing.

Although the writer-professor with whom I studied at this college was not then, as he is now, world famous, he definitely had charisma. There were about twelve students in his class—ten women and two men, if I remember correctly. The men can be dismissed at once. The ten women were all, by definition, exceptionally intelligent. For some unfathomable reason, most of them were also exceptionally beautiful. From the beginning of September until the end of June, all of us competed frantically to please the teacher.

Now, what does "competed frantically to please the teacher" mean? Well, it means that we used our minds and bodies to gain his approval, just as he used his to gain ours. We dressed in a certain way, talked in a certain way, wrote our short stories in a certain way, and walked into his office for our bi-monthly individual "conferences" in a certain way, each of us hoping against hope he'd recognize us as that very special person whose body and mind he could appreciate, admire, cherish and caress.

I won.

But then, I may not have been the only winner. Perhaps there were ten winners, and he was just prodigiously gifted at juggling his time schedule to include all of us. At college as in high school, I was an active subject rather than a passive object in my love affairs with professors. This time, though, I knew the person was not a crucial element in my destiny. Both of us felt fairly rotten about betraying our partners, and found the hotel rooms we resorted to at once expensive and shoddy. We soon phased out the erotic aspect of our friendship—and fortunately so, for had the other students become aware of it, the atmosphere in the classroom would probably have been affected. We stayed in touch, however, for a number of years afterward.

But now my story switches directions.

At the age of twenty, under the auspices of my excellent college, I came to Paris for my "junior year abroad," then went on to spend my senior year abroad, and to do a Master's degree abroad, and now, twenty years and two French children later, I have hit upon the perfect inscription for my tombstone: "Once abroad, always abroad."

Oddly enough, despite Frenchmen's worldwide reputation for being sexually obsessed, my dealings in France with professors, employers, gynecologists, dentists and shrinks have all been relatively maul-free. Since I did not become ugly overnight upon moving to Paris, I have gradually come to wonder whether my borderline erotic experiences as a young woman were not, at least partially, determined by cultural factors—i.e., whether there was not something specifically American (rather than, say, "modern" or "Western") about them. It seems to me that as a general rule (and with all the usual caveats regarding this sort of generalization), the French accept the fact that they have and are bodies. The prevailing social decorum is not as all-or-nothing as it is in the States, where the alternative seems to be: either overt sexual contact or feigned indifference to all physical characteristics. In France there is an intermediary level of communication based on the constant exchange of glances, witty remarks, hand gestures, and the like. Both men and women take part in this exchange. As the French do not attempt to radically rid social existence of physicality, they are not in such a state of patent contradiction and frustration as are the Americans (I think I'm mainly speaking of white Americans here). In a word, they tend to value the art of sublimation.

Americans, it would seem—again, these are the humble clumsy observations of a former insider and current outsider who has just spent a few perplexed months back on the "inside"—are taught less to love or enjoy their bodies than to take care of them. As a people, they seem to conceive physicality essentially in terms of health, exercise, self-defense, autonomy, anatomy, and how-to sex manuals. When one roams the aisles of the supermarkets from which they feed themselves, one essentially has the choice between health food and junk food; plain ordinary wonderful unprocessed unimproved unadulterated food is virtually impossible to find. Americans are becoming phobic about what they put into their bodies—no other country in the world diets so much or suffers from so many eating disorders. In the realm of eroticism, analogous extremes are represented by pornography and *The Joy of Sex*. It is as though the American people required that everything erotic and gastronomic be quantified, verbalized, exhaustively described and dissected and discussed.

As a result, they often seem genuinely (or disingenuously?) convinced that the whole aesthetic, interactive dimension of their bodies is non-existent. Taking this dimension into account can imply concealing as much as revealing, modesty as much as brazenness; it is the opposite of "letting it all hang out." I once had a beautiful young long-blonde-haired American female student who came close to getting herself lynched in Morocco by sauntering across a field wearing nothing but short shorts and a halter-top. A group of Arab peasants tore after her waving pitchforks—and she was not only terrified but totally nonplussed at the aggressiveness of their reaction to her body. She was just being natural! By European standards, beautiful young long-blond-haired American girls who stare men straight in the face are not natural, they are come-ons. By North African standards, they are prostitutes if not witches. No, I'm not defending the veil; I'm simply marveling at American lack of sensitivity to the fact that—and the manner in which—other people, other peoples, might respond to their bodies.

Sexual harassment, on the job and elsewhere, definitely exists in France, but that is not quite what I'm talking about here. I am talking, rather, about the way in which a certain degree of eroticism is not only tolerated on the social scene but considered to be a normal part of it. Like my own American students of today, I was enraged and humiliated, when I first came to Paris, by the stares, whistles and muttered remarks of men I passed in the streets. My first attempts to take pensive solitary walks in the cities of Southern Italy invariably ended in fits of hysteria and tears. But the native women in these countries know perfectly well how to handle their men. And the rape rates are far, far higher in the United States, where playful, tacit, intangible erotic exchange in public is increasingly taboo. (I still squirm whenever I recall the time, on a French TV-show with a number of other women writers, I was the only one who claimed she resented these unsolicited displays of male approval. The other guests were overtly nostalgic about the "good old days" when men used to whistle at them in the streets, though it wasn't quite clear whether these days had vanished because they had aged or because feminism had cowed men into silence.)

Admittedly, there have been occasions in France on which I've felt my beauty to be a handicap. Once or twice I've narrowly escaped rape; more than once or twice I've had devastating doubts about whether a person's enthusiasm for one of my books or articles might not be rightfully due to my big blue eyes. This has tended to make me insecure—and even, sporadically, miserable. But I refuse to exaggerate. These are small dramas. My beauty has never made me nearly as miserable as an assembly-line worker, or a crack addict, or a black mother on welfare.

I have also—calmly, naturally, as every beautiful woman knows how to do—allowed my beauty to bring me minor favours and advantages: faster service in restaurants, increased courtesy in libraries, more humorous and less expensive exchanges with policemen.... The occasions have literally been countless. They have also been unavoidable—to avoid them, I should have had to disguise myself as an ugly person (as did Simone Weil) by wearing thick black glasses and dressing in frumpy clothes, or indulging in some extreme "eating disorder."

Listen, I would like for once to lay all my cards on the table (I might as well—I'm a novelist now, which means I can be neither hired nor fired; in many important ways I have nothing to lose). Every human being on this earth is a combination of a mind and a body, an intelligence and a beauty, greater or lesser, now greater, now lesser, forever in flux and forever in interaction. But it is quite rare that one and the same person should experience both extremes, being treated alternately as all-body and as all-mind. Having exercised such wildly disparate professions as masseuse and feminist journalist, nude model and English professor, bar "hostess" and guest lecturer in prestigious universities, I am probably in a better position than most to revolt against the bad faith so prevalent in the United States today (since it cannot possibly be a question of naiveté), which pretends that our minds do not live in bodies, and that we respond to each other's minds independently of each other's bodies, and that what we love in each other when we make love to each other's bodies is not also, in large part, each other's minds, and that professors can teach and students study without their bodies ever being present in the classroom, and that bosses and employees and colleagues and workmates can interact professionally without their bodies ever being present in the office or factory—and that, moreover, it is possible for bodies to miraculously burst into existence when in private darkened bedrooms enclosing one or two or more consenting adults, all systems are suddenly said to be "go," whereas they have been forced to "stop" "stop" "stop" and "stop" all day long in every other situation in which they have found themselves.

These American bodies are no longer allowed to smoke, they are no longer allowed to joke, they are no longer allowed to smell; all of their sexy ambiguities have been banished to oblivion, war has been declared on their capacity for innuendo; flirting has been outlawed because it presupposes inequality (and this is true, or, more accurately, flirting underlines, renders flagrant and therefore undeniable, the inequality that in fact exists between the beautiful and the less beautiful, the intelligent and the less intelligent, the funny and the less funny)—oh at all costs let us not recognize these sorts of inequality, let us cover our eyes and pinch our noses and plug our ears in front of them; the work place is for getting work done and schools and universities are for getting an education and restaurants are for eating and bars are for drinking and streets are for striding purposefully from one place to another and none of these places no no no is an appropriate place for bodies, for sensuality, for sidelong glances, for flirting, ah ah ah, flirting leads to rape, the eyes and words of a man on a woman's body are already a miniature version of rape, and all forms of physical exchange between human bodies must be as predictable and safe and contractual as the sale of a house.

Again, let me attempt to be clear and discerning and calm. People who study well and write good papers, whether they are beautiful or ugly, brown or yellow, tall or short, should receive good marks; and people who have appropriate credentials or working records should never need to consent to being sodomized by the powers-that-be to get a job or a degree or a promotion. The role of beauty—and every other culturally or genetically inherited factor—in such situations as legal trials, political elections, thesis defenses and tenure hearings should be as close to zero as possible. (Thus, it is outrageous that Californians should currently be discussing the length of a judge's skirt: if judges and lawyers in many countries wear long black robes, it is precisely in order to annul or at least neutralize the particularities of their bodies.)

In public life, in other words, modern democratic institutions are rightly required to be blind to physical traits. At the opposite end of the spectrum there is love-making, in which physicality attains extremes of intensity. But in between the two there is social existence—life on the job, in the neighbourhood, at school, in the subway—a fascinating, shimmering, shifting mix of public and private, physical and spiritual, proximity and distance, conformity with code and spontaneous invention. What I am saying is that this crucial middle ground (of which, of course, physicality is but one of numerous aspects) is currently being eroded to nothingness, in the United States, by maniacal verbalization and ludicrous legalism. I'm saying that the compulsion to aberrant sexual behaviour is worsened, not attenuated, when sociality is thus unnaturally invaded by moral imperatives and declarations and calculations.

What I am not saying (I insist, politely banging my fist on the table) is, "Hey, Men! Hunting Season Open All Year!" All forms of sexual coercion are repulsive. But we must be careful or, under pretext of policing them, we shall lose a vast and rich dimension of human existence, namely the language of bodies, the hundred silent languages of bodies, which vary from country to country, social class to social class and milieu to milieu—yes, the complex, moving languages through which, wordlessly, endlessly, men and women ask and answer questions about each other, move, suggest, demur, wiggle, giggle, arch eyebrows, light cigarettes, graze a hand, a cheek, a shoulder blade, manifest wonder, admiration, tenderness, arousal, delight, defiance....(Is it because these languages are being silenced in America that gays and Lesbians so often resort to grotesquely obvious codes to get their messages of desire across?) But—ah ah ah and then, but then, what if desire becomes aggression? What if it becomes manipulation and threat and blackmail? What if it becomes forcing and pushing, shoving and battering, angry hell? Well then then then, if it becomes that, well then, there are already laws against that. But if it does not become that, then it becomes life. And the very definition of life is "You win a few, you lose a few." Since when does one go running to a lawyer or a journalist every time there is a loss?

What we have a right to in this life, as even the U.S. constitution acknowledges, is not happiness; it is, rather, the pursuit of happiness, which is a very different thing indeed. In the same way, the concept of equal rights in no way implies we are or must pretend to be identical to one another. If a deck of cards contains fifty-two fours of diamonds, what sort of passionate poker game will anyone be able to play?

My daughter is also turning out to be beautiful and intelligent which means that, in addition to teaching her to eschew boasting about it, I shall need to teach her a certain number of things about what sort of treatment she can expect at the hands of the world, just as parents have always prepared their children for the (positive and negative) effects of being Ukrainian, Tasmanian, Jewish, Catholic, dwarves, white, black, hemophilic, red-haired, skinny, knock-kneed, and so on and so forth, including all the possible combinations of these traits. Though they will have more or less weighty consequences depending on the geographical, historical, political, and social context in which one grows up, all these factors are part of the hand one is dealt at life's outset. There is no fatalism here; I don't mean that once you get your cards the game is tantamount to over. I simply mean that all of us play the game according to the cards we have in our hand—bluffing and feinting, discarding and drawing, trying to influence the other players, winning and losing....The progressive, liberal, revolutionary, existential philosophies we have espoused over the past couple of hundred years have tended to blind us to this simple truth, universally recognized by novelists and children: one deals with what is dealt.

BRIAN FAWCETT,
excerpts

Gender Wars

The material presented here is taken from a quirky book that mixes a novel with some position statements about the differing ways of men and women. We have excerpted a few of Fawcett's commentaries on gender differences. They are—some of them— explicit and, like Huston's remarks, unabashed and provocative. Like Huston, too, Fawcett is not afraid to explore some controversial territory. He sounds at times like a school teacher, at times like a philosopher and at other times like a gossip. What we couldn't do in editing Fawcett's work is give a sense of the way the two foci—novel and commentary—mix and mingle on the page, sometimes requiring the reader to turn pages back and forth.

Questions:

1. Compare Fawcett's and Huston's boldness in terms of style and content.
2. How does Fawcett present himself differently—as teacher, philosopher, gossip—from paragraph to paragraph?
3. The author ranges widely, too, from ancient to modern sources. Is this effective?
4. Would you say that both Fawcett and Huston appear, in their prose, to be egotistical?
5. Fawcett is polemical. What do you understand this term to mean?

Orgasms

Female orgasms are more important, interesting, and more variable than male orgasms. Everyone knows this by now, but yet an

amazing number of heterosexual women are in their late twenties before they take possession of this fact, and most men ignore it until late in their thirties. What a waste.
1. Common sense tells us that the best sex is the kind that engages the maximum number of our senses, and oral sex confirms this. Cunnilingus is easily the best and most reliable method of bringing a woman to orgasm, and for determining if, when, and how well she's having one. Contrary to legend, the male sex organ is a poor instrument of empirical or aesthetic judgement. It simply doesn't have enough nerve endings. A head-giver has a superior tactile, visual, and olfactory vantage point, and a human tongue has more interesting textures than a penis, finger, or vibrator. The intensity and variety of female orgasms appear to be relatively limitless, subject to a number of general factors:
   a. Direct and isolated stimulation of the clitoris produces intense, localized, and "high-frequency" orgasms that some women find painful. This variety is equally (and sometimes more easily) produced through digital stimulation or with vibrators. In most cases the clitoris emerges from subcutaneous tissue and becomes erect only with or shortly prior to orgasm, and both orgasm and clitoris rapidly subside. This variety of female orgasm is similar to male orgasm.
   b. A more indirect orgasm can occur if the labia and surrounding tissue are stimulated orally, or if oral play is coupled with interrupted penetration and copulation. The result (occasionally) is a labial and vaginal engorgement, along with greater, more gradual, and more long-lasting clitoral erection. Orgasms are longer lasting, more "low-frequency," and almost never painful, and subsequent intercourse is a wholly different and usually more pleasurable experience for both female and male.
2. Orgasms that coincide with labial and vaginal engorgement are probably the source of what some researchers have called the "vaginal orgasm." They can be explained physiologically with engorgement, nerve synapses in the engorged tissue re-circulate sensation, diffusing (and sometimes extending) it, and thus

the orgasm is more indirect than when surrounding tissues are not engorged. This is probably what latter-day sexologists mean when they talk about "G-spots." What seems to have eluded them is this: what produces a woman's orgasm is not so much a location but a carefully manufactured event that exists temporarily in a woman's mind and body—and in a man's head.
3. Labial engorgement is the physiological equivalent of male erection. (Vaginal engorgement has no male equivalent.)
4. A small percentage (ten percent?) of women experience spontaneous labial engorgement, while another ten to fifteen percent experience it during a "normal" penetrative intercourse (depending on a number of tactile and non-tactile factors). The size of a man's penis is fairly far down the list. Most women require five to fifteen minutes of skilled stimulation to achieve labial engorgement, even when the level of interpersonal intimacy and trust is very high. The most effective and pleasurable technique, again, is cunnilingus. Vaginal engorgement is rarer and seems to be a nexus of physical and psychological effects. If "female" mysteries exist (and they clearly do), this is one of them.
5. Some women, as a side effect of labial engorgement, exude aromas that can addict their partners for anywhere from twenty minutes to thirty years.

Male orgasms are fun, too. They're also a lot more variable than is generally recognized, particularly when they aren't confused with ejaculation. For some men, this variability comes with aging, because they learn that withholding an orgasm can be at least as much fun as getting it off and done with. Unfortunately, fear too often becomes a factor at this point, and the result is impotence.

Still, male orgasms are almost always less intense than the orgasms women have. A wise uncle once told me that St. Augustine took the following comparative measure:

If the measure of pleasure were divided into ten, nine would go to women, and one would go to men.

My wise uncle went on to suggest that men, mistaking an empirical calculation for a hostile political slogan, have historically responded to St. Augustine's formula by insisting on a nine-to-one orgasm numerical balance in their favour to even things out.

I reasoned that since Augustine was a saint, the versified measure he took (and who knows what was lost or added in the translation into English) was a theological truth and I didn't question it for many years. Now I think that the true ratio is about seven to three in favour of women, and I steer away from comparing the two kinds of orgasms. Between the two genders there is an infinity of individual pleasure gradients with so many contributory intangibles that only a fool would make a serious attempt to quantify them.

Women are capable of multiple orgasms within a single erotic encounter, while for most men orgasm terminates the encounter—often with extreme abruptness. In a sense, then, all male ejaculations are premature, and sensible men learn to pursue other erotic goals. Alas, sensible men are almost as rare as wise men, who treat the quality and intensity of their orgasms less as material for self-epiphany and more as an indicator to the quality of their treatment of their sexual partners.

Some other items concerning orgasm to ponder:

1. What *is* the point of a quick orgasm?
2. If the total number of female orgasms on the planet could be doubled or tripled, it would solve most, if not all, of the world's problems. Wars would cease, the general level of violence would diminish, sensible economic and political activities would flourish, and women and men would be infinitely happier. No, I'm not suggesting that women are the cause of our collective troubles. Men are. But if everyone made doubling and tripling female orgasm rates a priority, men would be spending too much time in bed to get into trouble. They wouldn't have time for war and other sublimations, and while they were in bed, they'd learn the sensible arts of compromise and conversation.

Okay, I know, I know—be practical. But if something so eminently sensible isn't practical, why isn't it?

Testosterone

Germaine Greer has described testosterone as a "race poison," by which I take her to mean that it is poisoning the human species from within. She's right, and my only criticism is that she doesn't pursue her insight far enough. Human males carry around massively excessive loads of it. It makes them violent, stupid, hairy, and bald, and it no longer has any offsettingly positive purpose. It is a dangerous drug that, left unchecked, will eventually exterminate us and destroy the planet along the way.

While we were still in the caves or in trees, testosterone provided human males with the aggression necessary to fight more powerful, larger or more numerous animals, and it helped stronger individuals breed successfully while natural selection was still a biological necessity. Short of the kind of protein-poor environment inhabited by the Yanomami in the Amazon, no human environment that I know of requires this degree of aggression and violence.

Civilization makes the human qualities engendered by testosterone vestigial and counter-productive. In the crowded quarters in which we live, the presence of excessive amounts of testosterone has created environments like the Bronx, Somalia, along with virtuals like the World Wrestling Federation and Pro Football. It precipitated the arms race, kept the Cold War spending us into bankruptcy, and it will be the true source of whatever geopolitical lunacies rain down on us in the near future. It's no accident that seventy percent of the acts of violence committed in North America are perpetrated by men between the ages of seventeen and twenty-four, when male testosterone levels are at their peak. It is the non-behavioural fuel behind male violence against women and children, the banana skin on the floor at every male intersection in the world. It is rape-plunder-Wheaties. If anything on this planet is going to survive, we're going to have to make a radical reduction in the amount of human testosterone circulating in it.

Am I being silly here? No. I'm completely serious about this. It takes very small amounts of testosterone to provide human beings with enough aggressive energy to get out of bed in the morning, and only a very little more for us to have a normal sex drive and act like decent people. About the amount that women have will do just fine. Both men and women produce small amounts of testosterone in the adrenal gland. The superfluous stuff males have is manufactured in the Leydig cells of the testicles, right next door to the also biologically superfluous sperm-producing cells.

Please relax. I'm not about to suggest general castration of our male population. But it's now common practice to regulate (allegedly for reasons of women's health and well-being—the kind that benefit males) the amount of progesterone and estrogen women have in their bodies. Why not regulate the levels of testosterone males carry? It would be extremely easy to justify the public and individual benefits. Crime rates would drop dramatically, sexual violence would become a rarity, warfare would become rarer still. Sure, razor blade and male hair-replacement sales would drop, the NHL, NFL, and a number of other blood sports would fall into a steep decline, and a few already insecure guys might feel more insecure because their balls are smaller and a little less bouncy to the touch. Small price to pay for survival of the species.

The problem, of course, is that no government could be trusted to regulate testosterone. They would turn testosterone into a political commodity, and we'd soon have a worse nightmare on our hands than the one we're currently trapped in—everyone in the Third World wandering around in a testosterone-free daze, testosterone-loaded armies and militias fighting in specialized war zones, bozos mainlining synthetic testosterone for the business and recreational advantages. Still, Greer is right when she says it's a poison and it is therefore only logical to at least make a public identification of testosterone, and perhaps even to invoke our education system to encourage sensible people to download their individual excesses.

Hygiene

For reasons of efficiency, most animals use the same body zone for sexual reproduction and for waste removal. Since human beings are among the few species that fiddle with one another's genitals for the sheer fun of it, efficient animal design can present aesthetic problems and may even be a design flaw. What I'm saying here, in a roundabout way, is that the practice of personal hygiene is an important part of human sexual pleasure.

Okay, I know the counter-arguments. If there had been a few showers in ancient Judaea, the Song of Solomon never would have been written, and the perfume industry never would have got off the ground. But there's another way to see this. A rutting bull moose is drawn to a cow moose by the scent of very specific hormones, not to the fecal detritus attached to the mating thereabouts. And it is difficult to deny that if personal hygiene had been a common practice in the ancient world, there would have been a lot more fucking, more oral sex, more female orgasms, and a whole lot less fighting and killing. Let's face it. Except for a tiny, strange minority, there's nothing erotic about lousy hygiene.

It has always astonished me that so many women—and, I'm reliably informed by my women friends, even more than by men—are so careless about hygiene. Since erotic pleasure operates by its own dynamic rules and not those of factory production lines, political debates, or abattoirs, it seems like common sense to start erotic encounters at olfactory neutral, and to let it power up by the specific olfactory secretions of arousal. From that point, artifice can blossom as each of us chooses, and the blossoms will be larger, finer, and better perfumed.

Personally, I like a moderate degree of artifice. There is no olfactory nexus more pleasant and eroticizing than the illumination of vaginal aromas and secretions through expensive French perfume. Other people may prefer baby powder, tomato paste, pine needles, axle grease, or even cleaning fluids. I've heard of couples who like to roll around in horse manure while they're screwing, and we've all heard about occupational aids affecting olfactory incitements—it explains the popularity of high colonics among members of the medical profession, and high incidence of golden showers and glass coffee-table defecation routines in the upper echelons of the legal community.

I can't say if this is true of males, but each human female body generates a signature aroma under the genial stress of sexual activity, and a man who doesn't pay close attention to these is an inadequate lover, a sensory moron, and a fool. I have a theory that it is possible to tell what is happening to a woman—even to discover her specific and essential sexual character—by her scent alone. Likewise, sexual dysfunctions and ambivalences are also recognizable from hygiene and olfactory conditions and attitudes. In my experience, erotic ambivalence in women invokes a scent and taste that distinctly resemble that of copper sulfate. Similarly, the range of musks women produce is extraordinarily variable. In some women it can smell like woodsmoke, while in others it is cut with the scent of milk. Others give off a faintly vinegary scent. Bacterial presences, mild or endemic, also influence sexual aromas, as do deodorants, which I happen to dislike intensely because they are aimed simply at paralyzing the sensorium.

One more note. Clinical hygiene is more important in casual sexual relationships (and in stable but marginal relationships) than for people in the early stages of a love affair (or in any stage of a Grand Passion). This is because the beloved (male or female) exudes an addictive substance that grows more characteristic and powerful after it has rested in or on the body. This is why people who are deeply in love often like to make love in the late afternoon or in the early morning, while most long-term and casual affairs are most satisfactorily consummated late in the evening, after bathing.

Race

AN AMERICAN LITERARY and cultural critic, Henry Louis Gates, Jr., often puts the word "race" in italics; he does this to draw attention to its social and constructed—rather than its supposedly "natural"—aspects. That Canadian writers are also concerned with how race is both read and performed the following articles make abundantly clear. Indeed, other selections in *Changing Identities*—notably karen/miranda augustine's study of sexuality and race, as well as Gamal Abdel-Shehid's piece on race and sports—examine this issue despite their placement elsewhere in this reader. Rinaldo Walcott is another writer whose work might interest you in this regard; his *Black Like Who?* is an incisive study of race and Canadian music. Moreover, "black studies" as an academic field has flourished recently. Among other practices it has scrutinized and caused to be reformulated are literary criticism (insofar as which books should be regarded as canonical and how texts of all kinds should be studied) and the writing of history.

SHAHNAZ KHAN

"The Space Beneath My Feet"

As she mentions early in this preface to her book on Muslim women in the so-called Western world, Shahnaz Khan's project

CHANGING IDENTITIES

has matured for more than ten years, but has gained in urgency because of the events of September 11, 2001. *Aversion and Desire* is both a broad-based academic study and a poignant account of specific Muslim women, their experiences and personal narratives, in the diaspora. The preface offers a more specific situating of Khan herself. Self-identified as "a muslim feminist academic," she confronts the questions and debates that motivated and affected her rather than the women she interviewed for the book.

Questions:

1. Issues of representation, of who gets to speak for whom, are important to Khan. Why is this important not only to Khan, but also to other writers in *Changing Identities*?
2. What is the binary thinking that Khan resists in her preface?
3. Khan writes, "the category muslim is fluid, mobile and shifting." How does this help us understand the constructed rather than the essential character of identity?
4. How do Khan's accounts of the period following September 11, 2001, conflict with much of what has appeared in the mainstream media?
5. Many of the women interviewed in *Aversion and Desire* reveal a great deal to Khan. What in the preface gives the sense that Khan is a researcher to be trusted with personal stories?

This book is about negotiating a space for women who either self-identify as muslim or are coded by others as such. And post-September 11, 2001 has reinforced the urgent need for such a third space which identifies women's resistance to stereotypical pre-determinations of being muslim. Through this space their accounts suggest hybridized negotiations and generate possibilities for a politics of difference within the category muslim.

As this paperback edition of my book goes to print, I am, with urgency, reminded why I began this project ten years ago. At the time I had been working toward a doctoral dissertation on employment opportunities (or lack thereof) for South-Asians in Canada. As the United States drifted into the Gulf War, I found that as a muslim feminist I had no platform from which to speak and make my objections about the war known.

Dominant analysis of the events contained increased rhetoric about Islam spawning a monolithic civilization that had not embraced modernity and to which the muslim-as-savage-other belonged. Media events depicted muslim men (as embodied by Saddam Hussein) intent on waging war against the civilized world—read: the West. Although the laws of the Iraqi regime did not require women to cover up, conventional ideas about the plight of shrouded muslim women victimized by muslim men surfaced frequently. These images and accompanying text suggested yet again Gayatri Spivak's famous phrase about westerners' need to save brown women from brown men. And I screamed silently that I was muslim and did not need to be rescued.

Moreover, the savagery of the third world man, in this case the Arab man, denied him rights over his own land and its resources and condemned his country to a bombing campaign. This military action was led by the only superpower of the new world order, as George Bush (the elder) reminded us again and again. Although Bush was careful not to use the term savage when referring to muslims, he did use similar terms to speak about Saddam Hussein. The media happily resorted to old stereotypes to provide visual imagery and commentary that nevertheless reconfirmed these ideas about all muslims. And public imagination filled in all the necessary blanks.

The debate surrounding the Gulf War did not raise questions about imperialism's need for a supply of cheap oil. Instead what was debated again and again was the role religion plays in Islamic societies and the place of women in Islam. Multiculturalist paradigms that frequently recognize and promote static notions of monolithic muslim communities support this kind of debate.

Many of the teach-ins that followed and the panel discussions that were held were about the only issue deemed important to the people of the region: religion. The forums often turned into Islam 101, a quick course on understanding the meaning of true Islam. Many muslims in North America, myself included, were compelled to counteract the misinformation about Islam with our version of "what Islam really says." Such articulations reinforced the muslim-equals-religion equation and revealed to me the very lack of tangible space from which to practice progressive politics within the category muslim. In other words I wanted to speak to the issues that arose from the contradictions of being forced into either an orientalist attack on Islam or a defense of it.

I did not find such a space among feminists either. As I claimed my voice as a muslim, I found I was being slotted into positions not of my making. Many feminists were happy to hear me condemn Islam and muslim men—a venture for which they were willing to provide full support. Others wanted me to do theological scholarship and speak to the ways in which a reading of the sacred texts of Islam might support women's rights. Although I applaud feminist theologian Riffat Hasan when she does this work, it is not my agenda. I am more interested in examining how religion, along with race, class and sexuality, functions as a fundamental organizing principle of women's lives in diasporic space. Although American feminists, including Yvonne Haddad, Minoo Moallam and Laila Ahmed, have worked toward creating such a space, it is different in Canada. I have found that I often stand in a vacuum.

It is now November 2001. The dominant media tell us that the world has changed. Has it? The world is not the United States. The fear and uncertainty that grip the United States have been around for hundreds of years in other parts of the world. War, destruction of cities, fear and pestilence have affected Asia, Africa, South America and to a lesser extent Europe. People have lived in fear that their children might not come home from school, that their house may be bombed during the day (or night) or that their loved ones might be the victims of snipers. These people have lived in places that include Vietnam, Cambodia, Kosovo, Sierra Leone, Colombia, Palestine and Lebanon. In recent years United States imperialist foreign policy has helped create the conditions for these events in much of the world. And now the world has come to the United States. American foreign policy has boomeranged.

Not much has changed in terms of the nature of the violence and the loss of innocent lives since the 1991 Gulf War. These unhappy events continue unabated. However, in 2001 the arena has changed. The September 11, 2001, attacks are unprecedented as they are attacks on "the centre of the empire." And they have unleashed a tremendous amount of destruction. Internationally they have unleashed a military massacre of mythical proportions. No matter how often they tell me, I cannot and will not use the word war for what is going on in Afghanistan. People weary of decades of conflict, facing drought, living in a country filled with land mines are being bombed day and night. Their plight demonstrates a chilling disregard for non-American lives in the West. Their crime: They happen to be ruled by a regime that they did not elect but that came to power as a result of United States foreign policies, a project in which they were aided and abetted by Saudi Arabia and Pakistan.

The attacks also have repercussions domestically. Freedom and democracy, it appears, will henceforth be secured through increased surveillance and overriding of taken-for-granted liberties, such as the right to privacy and due process. Laws are being enacted that erode civil liberties and give police and intelligence agencies sweeping powers to arrest and monitor people. Ordinary people's freedom to criticize and demonstrate against the government will likely be compromised with the exercise of these powers by the state. I suspect that the increasing crackdown on anti-globalization demonstrations will accelerate further at the next round of meetings, where protestors might come up against the brutal fist of the state. Economically we have seen huge sums of money diverted to strengthen security and earmarked for defense budgets. We are told that we are back in the days of deficit financing and will likely see spending cuts to social services. In their desire for security against terrorism, a fearful citizenry appears poised to support these measures.

There is another aspect of this fear that is spreading across North America. Underlying racism against muslims and Arabs has blossomed into open rhetoric about "the clash of civilization" thesis which draws up and reinforces binary thinking. An article under this title was written by Samuel Huntington and appeared in a 1993 issue of *Foreign Affairs*. Writing shortly after the Gulf War, Huntington argued that the fundamental conflict in the coming years would not be ideological or economic. It would be cultural. This conflict, he concluded, would be between nations with different civilizations and he identified Islam and the West as the two major actors. Huntington proposed that the West needed to strengthen its military capacity in order to fend off its enemies. So in essence, Huntington's clash of civilization thesis pits West versus the rest, particularly Islam.

Even people who do not subscribe to the racism that fuels binary thinking end up in political positions similar to Huntington's. For many people speak of the need to "tolerate" or respect those with different cultures. These views promote an understanding of cultures as distinct and unrelated, placed in a hierarchical relationship. Such a binary marks whites, the civilized race, as different from the violent and barbaric non-whites. Media statements support these positions. *The Globe and Mail* columnist William Johnson states, for example, that "Muslims have disproportionately been involved in violence." Such disparaging remarks are not limited to muslims alone. All non-white people are suspect. Another *Globe and Mail* columnist identifies those working in airport security as "immigrants, many of whom have backgrounds in countries that support terrorism." These comments reinforce the notion that "those" people working at airports (who are frequently non-white) cannot be trusted. Civilians suspected by virtue of their culture are judged and condemned; in recent days people have been threatened, beaten, killed and terrorized because they are deemed different and, therefore, dangerous. Mosques have been identified as places where dangerous people gather and, as such, have been subjected to threats and attacks. The fury, however, has not been limited to muslim places of worship. Temples and gurdwaras have also been targeted, reinforcing the conflation of muslims and non-whites as the demonic other.

Recent individual acts of violence directed at non-whites have another face, systemic violence carried on by the state. For binary thinking also manifests itself in rationales provided for increasing racist determination of immigration procedures (such as drawing up a list of countries from which applications will be scrutinized more than others). Moreover, recent changes in Canadian immigration policies prohibit students from countries on the terrorism watch list, such as Iran, Iraq and Libya, from taking courses in biology and chemistry. These policies suggest that people need to be cautious of the alien within. And externally the aliens need to be routed out in their homes, "or caves" as one United States official put it recently. Military action is thus sanctioned against those not yet judged according to due process but condemned through a manufactured paranoid hysteria. And I use the word "manufactured" because although anti-muslim and anti-non-white sentiments draw upon continuously recurring themes, the current fervor is also nurtured by remarks by world leaders such as Tony Blair and George Bush who speak about the need to secure freedom and democracy through state action. These comments suggest that any country that the United States thinks is a threat risks a bombing campaign—for it has been said again and again by Bush and other members of his government, "Either you are with us or against us."

There are some dissimilarities in 2001, however, from the frequent commentary about muslims and Arabs in 1991. There was little discussion of the issues in the jingoism surrounding the Gulf War. And western leaders leading the bombing raids against Iraq did not speak about the need to make distinctions between those who planned and carried out the invasion of Kuwait and those who did not. Nor was there any realization of the nature and extent of hate crimes that swept across North America against local residents of Arab descent or against those coded as muslim. This time it is a little different. Although support of the bombing of Afghanistan dominates mainstream media, there also appears to be some room for the growing analysis of the causes of the current crisis. And both Bush and Blair have spoken out against the increasing incidents of hate crimes. Likely their comments stem from a need to keep the coalition against terrorism intact and from an awareness of the voting power of muslims and Arabs at home. Perhaps they are also aware of the growing voices of dissent that have emerged from the anti-poverty and anti-globalization protests that have gained ground worldwide.

There is another aspect of this binary thinking. Globalization and militarization continue to contribute to massive impoverishment of the world's peoples. The sense of hopelessness arising from ecological disasters and urbanization exacerbates this poverty. People dislocated by war and political repression find themselves in what many social scientists refer to as a crisis of modernity. They frequently turn to simple solutions provided by particular readings of religion. This is certainly true in the case of political Islam or Islamism. These Islamist readings of religion promote absolute assertion of particular interpretations of the sacred and disregard others. The Islamist prophets, for instance Osama bin Ladin, do not derive their wide appeal from their knowledge of religion. They distort tradition and are mainly concerned with mobilizing people for their cause and with acquiring power, not with religious scholarship. Their rhetorical demands for justice, in what they perceive as an unjust world, become a salve for the wounded sensibilities of the disenfranchised in many muslim societies. Their call for a pure and authentic muslim society (the parameters of which only they determine) inverses the racist binary thinking found in western societies. These Islamist views also feed the clash of civilization thesis. For they claim that Islam is in danger and call for a holy war against America, christians, jews, westernized muslims, or just anyone who opposes them.

In my desire to identify the call for an authentic muslim society promoted by Islamists I do not in any way mean to say that their call for a pure society has the same power as the call for freedom and justice by the West. Instead I want to identify how notions of authenticity and morality are used to promote the self and exclude and vilify others. This is not an equal call for action. The West clearly has a military advantage. It can promote its terror through "legitimate" acts of war, mobilizing its military and coercing its allies in muslim societies to do the same, while the terror that Islamists advocate is manifested in guerrilla tactics like that of the bombing in New York (if indeed they are the force behind the September 11 attacks). Innocent civilians are killed in both calls to produce authentic and moral societies.

Space of Possibility

In post-September 11, Islam versus the West is a major manifestation of the binary thinking that polarizes the world. But it is also a time, I believe, for a larger conversation about the social inequalities that create and perpetuate dichotomies. I began this conversation 10 years ago with the intent to find a space where I could speak as a muslim feminist without either being pulled into the orientalist trap of racist disavowal of Islam or the Islamist call for true authenticity. Instead I wanted to examine how religion had contributed to creating the space (or lack thereof) in which I lived and spoke. My efforts have had a range of responses. First of all many muslims saw my work as a way to resolve their own dilemmas which they conceptualized in religious terms. They were unhappy with my continued emphasis on the social and wanted me to restrict my analysis to examine what is it that Islam really says and how that message relates to their lives in the diaspora. Some were quite resistant to my discussions of fluidity and shifting categories of muslim identity and particularly unhappy with my desire to include sexuality as an aspect of muslim identity.

Some feminists were also resistant to my work. Even those feminists who considered themselves anti-racist and critical race theorists frequently did not support my position. Some called me an orientalist. Others commented that my work was essentialist, that is, I was drawing upon perceived inherent qualities to discursively organize the category muslim woman. One woman of muslim background claimed that I was trying to set myself up as the authentic voice of the muslim female and, thus, all that I said was suspect. As I respond to these comments, I am aware that the category muslim is fluid, mobile and shifting and I do not aim to contain it within boundaries of my making. Instead I draw upon Gayatri Spivak's notion of strategic essentialism and thus enter the debate about the forces that organize the world in fundamental ways. For entering the category muslim helps me claim my voice and find a space for myself in Canada.

At the moment this space feels very narrow. Afghanistan, decimated by decades of war and drought, is being bombed into the Stone Age. In November 2001 (like in 1991) there are few forums to discuss the effects of imperialist policies in the world. Instead the issue of what religion says is raised continuously. How do we understand Islam and women's place in Islam so that we might understand and tolerate these very different people? Shades of the clash of civilization argument lurk in these sentiments. Indeed in recent anti-war forums, feminists of muslim background who speak out against the conflict in Afghanistan and the racism it has spawned in the diaspora find they are pressured to assume apologetic positions around Islam. For the terrain of the debate has shifted to the religious frame, what Islam says and what it does not say. Moreover they find it a struggle to be heard as muslim unless they wear the *hejab* or defer to the imam. Many people do not want to hear from or about muslim women (or indeed women of colour) unless they situate themselves as victims and subservient to their men. Vilification of Sunera Thobani as she critiqued United States foreign policy identifies how little space Canada affords outspoken women of colour.

I believe that disruption of binaries including the sacred and secular Islam and the West provides a path out of this dilemma.

Destabilizing dichotomous thinking allows us to examine how these seemingly polar opposites are interconnected in complex and contradictory ways. Muslim identity can be viewed as heterogeneous and shifting, freeing us from the predetermined boundaries in which we are continuously confined. Homi Bhabha's notion of hybridization in the third space reinforces this disruption and identifies translations of sedimented culture into shifting sites of knowledge and experience. Within this third space, muslim subjectivity is no longer about an identity politics making claims about absolute knowledge boxed in rigid boundaries, an identity that a few can control (such as Islamists) and others can vilify (such as orientalists). And the unstable, hybridized muslim identity is no longer a trait to be transcended but a productive tension filled with possibility. And the possibilities are endless.

At this moment when binary thinking about other cultures fuels military policy and risks annihilation of whole societies, understanding the hybridized lives of muslim women in this manuscript helps identify these possibilities. Their accounts resist easy explanations and challenge generalizations about muslim women's lives. And their lives refuse to be contained within predetermined boundaries. Instead their narratives suggest shifting and mobile strategies and remind us that the women's lives in Canada are situated at the intersection of race, class, gender, sexuality and religion. Their stories remind us that the East and West, muslim and christian, us and them are not ontological absolutes. But, rather, these binaries rest uneasily on interlocking categories. Within such a space we may begin to move beyond dichotomous thinking and examine lives as they are lived in the social and political context in which people are situated.

The women's accounts suggest ways of destabilizing static notions of identity and illuminate a way out of the debilitating space of inaction. Yet documenting hybridized lives is not sufficient in mobilizing for social action. For the subaltern strategies embedded within the women's narratives do not attempt to overthrow state power. However, their accounts of hybridized lives do generate the possibility of progressive action within the category muslim. Women who refuse to be limited in what they do, what they wear, what they say and who they love can claim voice as muslim within diasporic space in the West. And they can help forge solidarity with other local and international progressive groups in order to mobilize against injustice and political, economic and social inequality.

MOUSTAFA BAYOUMI,

"MY Passport, MY Self"

This essay was written six years before the events of September 11, 2001. That this is so makes the essay utterly astonishing to read. Written in response to the *1993* bombing in the World Trade Center, *before* its destruction resulting from the suicidal missions of 2001, "MY Passport, MY Self" presents Bayoumi's dilemma. Whenever he flies, he is regarded suspiciously because he fits the profile of an "Arab terrorist." More than simply a recording of his frustrations, this article explores the roots of...otherness, of immigration, of Islamic immigrants. Despite its brevity, "MY Passport, MY Self" speaks to the frightening power states—specifically the U.S.A.—that have to decide who are the guilty and how they should be punished.

Questions:

1. Bayoumi's sentence structure, his use of incomplete sentences: what end does this tactic serve?
2. The citation of Ibn Khaldun: why does Bayoumi introduce this fourteenth-century Arab scholar?
3. The reference to Rodney King, a black man whose beating by white members of the Los Angeles police precipitated a "race riot": is this allusion a valuable one or does it dilute Bayoumi's focus?

4. The strong motif of movement/immobility—e.g., the references to cabs, cab-drivers, sedentary peoples, etc.: does this unify the essay?
5. Bayoumi's reminiscences of his mother and *her* life, especially in Egypt: is this "personal touch" important in giving "MY Passport, MY Self" a more intimate feel?

I fear flying. The reason is simple and it has nothing to do with a fear of the air or of being airborne. In a sense I was myself air born, my parents both coming from Egypt, and me being born in Switzerland, then transplanted to Canada, now studying in the United States. My fear remains on the ground, neither sacred nor sublime. It rests on those points of departure, within those little private cities that spot the globe, on the outskirts of major centers. *If you are suspected long enough of something, you will eventually believe yourself guilty of it.* In a Western airport—those are the airports I know best—I am the itinerant terrorist. I do not know exactly when this metamorphosis takes place, whether it occurs somewhere on the way, in the train or the taxi, or with my first step into the airport (often through wall-less doors of metal-detecting equipment). Or perhaps it occurred sometime earlier, during the 1970s, entering my body like a dormant and undetected virus, only to bloom with my facial hair. Regardless, it has arrived (and continues to arrive) at unscheduled times and with all the extra baggage that such an arrival portends.

What then does it matter, say, what passport I have? Identities are even easier to counterfeit than passports. My passport marks me nationally (I am what they call a naturalized citizen), but those sly security folk at airports know that names reveal a far deeper nature than passports ever will. And if the name falls blandly flat (they too can be naturalized and neutralized), take a good look at the face. I must admit, I don't often remember *their faces*, the whiteness usually only reflecting the garish airport lighting, and I can only speculate what they remember of mine. Their expressions, though, remain. It is a little drama that is played out every time, with varying degrees of melodrama (different countries, after all, produce different schools of acting) but repeated so often as to produce and reproduce its own absurd theater of cruelty. The movement to suspicion is something I've so often seen now that if I don't fall victim to it, I become suspicious.

February 26, 1993. An explosion tears into the concrete fabric of lower Manhattan. Unforeseen, unprecedented, this event in the social fabric of corporate America threatens the media machine's ability to produce information and to monopolize the production of meaning. The event is itself charged with too much meaning, too little information. Anyone could have done it, for too many reasons. Within minutes multiple meanings are thrown into circulation—Serbians, Palestinians, Bosnians—but the lack of one singular meaning means no meaning is being produced at all. For the moment.

The radical quality of the event is evident at the time of its happening, before it becomes history, when it is still in a kind of pre-mediated state. Here, too much information does not destroy meaning; rather, there are too many cracks in the shell, pressure points giving way to the lies our state tells us. Their profound disruption comes not so much from their violence as from their element of surprise. The producers of meaning are surprised and are caught with their pants down. The system will have to work overtime, producing meaning (narratives, characters, histories) out of an event in order to compensate for their lack of prescience and power.

It happened almost a year before, in L.A., when a spark erupted into a fire that burned away all the fat around the lies and deception of one of our systems of social control—the justice system. A year later in L.A. when the verdicts were handed down, the system desperately tried to regain its ability to pass judgment, instead of being the object upon which judgment is passed. The state expects a rebellion with the new verdict. But the state once again merely shows its own inability to comprehend the power of rebellion. Once the state can expect something, it is back in control. But for the moment—before the analysis—a bomb explodes. Communities rebel. Too many causes for their effects. Six people die tragic deaths. Other minority communities suffer. In the meantime, all the King's horses and all the King's men will do all they can to put the production of meaning in their hands again.

Who are the victims of the WTC bombing? Certainly the most immediate victims belong to the class of new immigrants, some of the fatalities belonging directly to this class: new immigrants as hotel-workers, drawn to the imperial metropole for their livelihood. But even after the event new immigrants suffer. The surreptitious nature of an event like this virtually authorizes the state in all its royal machinery to create its own enemies at will. We were not let down. The industry of manufacturing the enemy (a highly lucrative field in this country) was able to produce an astonishing narrative of suspicion, whose players lurked in shadowy corners of storefront *masjids,* conferenced in lower-class apartment blocks, and hidden nests of hatred in unassimilated facial hair.

Like rats, everything about this cast of characters was dark, hidden, and, like the bomb explosion site, underground. At least since the Gulf War, we know that this underground quality marks it as separate from the royal machinery. This has little to do with firepower and even less to do with morality, but it has everything to do with perspective. The royal machinery looks from the top down like the hundreds of thousands of sorties flown over Iraq during the War, and this perspective becomes valorized. A way of viewing the world. For others, perspective is limited to those things beside oneself, in greater and greater circles but with no vanishing point. To look from top down or from bottom around—these are the options. To be a helicopter or a taxi cab. To be a hawk or a mole.

This is not just about movement, not even about the speed of movement, but about the place of movement. Both immigrants and imperial states are masters at manipulating the machinery of movement, yet their paths rarely cross as they fly at different altitudes. Who would have understood this but Ibn Khaldun, the fourteenth-century Arab Muslim scholar of social formations and philosopher of history. Social organization exists in many stages for Ibn Khaldun, with the Bedouin or nomadic being opposite to the sedentary lifestyle. His marvelous and secular mind is able to process so many events of social organization into an understanding of the codes of civilization—with neither prejudice nor sentimentality (though with a guiding sense of morality).

The sedentary propensity for luxury attracts with it the desire for scholars and their various jewels—like Ibn Khaldun himself (very aware of the conditions which gave him the opportunity to write), like the opportunity for my more tarnished musings here—in order that they may give some legitimacy to the royal machinery. But their growing desire for luxuries and false legitimation will ultimately spell their decline. Dynasties, royal machineries, state formations all come and go: yet all operate under a set of codes which are continually expanding in order to underwrite the existence of a social formation that is being *undermined* by its very growth and arrogance.

New immigrants watch carefully all sides of the road. They take hurried naps only when they are together in company or when they are in the saddle. That is, when they don't have a fare. Low to the ground, in constant movement, almost all New York City cab drivers are from the new immigrant class (though let's not fall into a position of liberal guilt, where all new immigrants become cab drivers). Our cast of characters has its own share of cab drivers, something which perhaps strikes fear into many. My cab driver, a terrorist? But immigrants, refugees, exiles understand movement differently than do the sedentary peoples. For the sedentary, movement is walking with a mobile phone, movement is the walkman, movement is only a fax of a movement. Within days of the WTC bombing, AT&T announced that temporary offices and special phone lines were established in order not to incapacitate the silent machinations of electronic capital (not in so many words). The idea of the twin towers has now become a total farce, their closure barely affecting any change in the flows of capital. At one point they indicated the end of competition; now, in addition, they're virtually just a nostalgic reminder of those days of movement: movement of capital, movement of people. Architecture as the site of congregating has become passé.

In the sedentary world, movement has become something almost purely symbolic or purely terrifying: politicians travel for no real purpose, tourists travel in memory of colonialism and in hopes of placing themselves on postcards. Armies, which at one time seemed almost obsolete with long-range nuclear missile technology, have become today's travelers.

Opposite these movements are the movements of immigrants, refugees, exiles. No wonder they drive you round and around the city. They know how to move a life.

I am looking at a picture of my mother, dated June 23, 1956. A significant date. Significant not only because it was exactly one month before Gamal Abdul-Nasser nationalized the Suez Canal. (War would come later, and my mother told me how she and all her classmates in the school of pharmacology wanted to do something to help and worked as voluntary nurses in the hospitals around Cairo—working for the new nation, caring for the wounded.)

In this picture, my mother is a scant twenty years old. Younger than I am now. There is another woman in the photograph, behind my mother, waiting her turn, shrouded in widow's black. My mother, at the table, in dark glasses and rolled up sleeves, is writing on a piece of paper. She tells me, "This small photo documents the first time women had the vote in Egypt." My mother, in Upper Egypt, voting on a forgotten referendum in the constitution. Eight men, some of them in suits and ties, most wearing the more traditional *gellabaya*, are watching the two women vote.

Egypt in the fifties. A popular coup d'etat looking for legitimation in the ballot box. The men in the suits are most likely outsiders to the region, government officials overseeing the election. Everything is coded in this picture. A coexistence between traditional ways and Western ways. Some observers may want to see the juxtaposition between my mother and the widow as that between the West and Islam; just take a look at the clothes. Yet each of these women is doing nothing but adapting herself to all the codes around, both new and old. A society in transition, everything in Egypt at this moment is being contested. But this is hardly unique to new nations. All societies are in a constant state of flux, the contestations between codes and values a daily phenomenon.

Structures of authority exist in order to lay order, to produce the codes by which things make sense. The state, organized religions, as well as university seminars all rationalize their orthodoxy. I can well believe that a certain kind of Islam can produce, as can all orthodoxies, a rational code in order to produce what is in effect an irrational event. And after the fact? More rationally, refining of codes and definitions. What a refusal of living!

Don't bother looking for me after you have read this. You won't find me. I will be spying on those dangerous imams with the brilliant sight of an eagle: I will be growling with the voice of a lion at the border guards; I will be licking injuries of the wounded with my rough and salty tongue. I will be prowling against your codes, and will jump without any warning.

WAYSON CHOY,
excerpt

Paper Shadows

A few years ago, editor Jim Wong-Chu's *Many-Mouthed Birds* appeared. The accounts of Chinese Canadian writers articulating their diverse experiences of adaptation, assimilation and alienation, it contains more than a few references to "paper children"—children claimed as family members in order to gain immigrant status. Wayson Choy, a prize-winning novelist, learned that he, too, fit that category; then he wrote the memoir, excerpts of which follow. Canada/China, adoptive mother/"real" mother: these motifs are woven together beautifully, elegiacally, by Choy. Memory, too, plays an important role here, augmenting the poignancy of the piece.

Questions:

1. Note the impact frequent brief paragraphs have on the pace of the excerpt. Is this technique a good one?
2. One could call the sections that make up the entire selection "vignettes." Discuss their effectiveness: in what writing situations are they appropriate?
3. How is the child's point-of-view presented?
4. Is the dialogue recollection or invention? When does it work best?
5. The beginning is simple and "electric." How is this achieved?

"I saw your mother last week."

The stranger's voice on the phone surprised me. She spoke firmly, clearly, with the accents of Vancouver's Old Chinatown: "I saw your *mah-ma* on the streetcar."

Not possible. This was 1995. Eighteen years earlier I had sat on a St. Paul's Hospital bed beside Mother's skeletal frame while she lay gasping for breath: the result of decades of smoking. I stroked her forehead and, with my other hand, clasped her thin, motionless fingers. Around two in the morning, half-asleep and weary, I closed my eyes to catnap. Suddenly, the last striving for breath shook her. I snapped awake, conscious again of the smell of acetone, of death dissolving her body. The silence deepened; the room chilled. The mother I had known all my life was gone.

Eighteen years later, in response to a lively radio interview about my first novel, a woman left a mysterious message: URGENT WAYSON CHOY CALL THIS NUMBER.

Back at my hotel room, message in hand, I dialed the number and heard an older woman, her voice charged with nervous energy, insist she had seen my mother on the streetcar.

"You must be mistaken," I said, confident that this woman would recognize her error and sign off.

"No, no, not your mother"—the voice persisted—"I mean your *real* mother."

"My first *crazy*," I remember thinking. *The Jade Peony* had been launched just two days earlier at the Vancouver Writers' Festival, and already I had a crazy. My agent had, half-whimsically, warned me to watch out for them. The crazies had declared open season upon another of her clients, a young woman who had written frankly of sexual matters. I was flattered, but did not really believe that my novel about Vancouver's Old Chinatown could provoke such perverse attention. Surely, my caller was simply mistaken.

"I saw your *real* mother." The voice emphatically repeated the word "real" as if it were an incantation.

My *real* mother? I looked down at the polished desk and absently studied the Hotel Vancouver room-service menu. My real mother was dead; I had witnessed her going. I had come home that same morning eighteen years ago and seen her flowered apron folded precisely and carefully draped over the kitchen chair, as it had been every day of my life. I remember quickly hiding the apron from my father's eyes as he, in his pyjamas and leaning on his cane, shuffled into the kitchen. Seeing that the apron was missing from the chair, he began, "She's ...?" but could not finish the question. He stared at the back of the chair, then rested his frail eighty-plus years against me. Unable to speak, I led him back to his bed.

The voice on the hotel phone chattered on, spilling out details and relationships, talking of Pender *Gai*, Pender Street, and noting how my novel talked of the "secrets of Chinatown."

I suddenly caught my family name, pronounced distinctively and correctly: *Tuey*. Then my grandfather's, my mother's, and my father's formal Chinese names, rarely heard, sang into my consciousness over the telephone.

"Those are your family names?" the voice went on.

"Yes, they are," I answered, "but who are you?"

"Call me Hazel," she said.

She had an appointment to go to, but she gave me a number to call that evening.

"Right now, I can't tell you much more."

"Oh," I replied lamely, "I understand."

I did not understand. I meant it as a pause, a moment in which to gather my thoughts. I wanted to learn more. Provoked and confused, I said what came immediately into my head:

"Where should I begin?"

The line went dead. Hazel was gone.

That afternoon, in my fifty-seventh year, a phone call from a stranger pushed me towards a mystery. The past, as I knew it, began to shift.

When I think of my earliest memories, I do not worry about family history, nor do I think of the *five-times-as-hard* hard times my parents endured.

I think, instead, of first hauntings.

At the age of four, something vivid happened to me. I woke up, disturbed by the sound of a distant clanging, and lifted my head high above the flanneled embankment that was my mother's back to see if a ghost had entered the room. Mother rolled her head, mouth partially open, sound asleep. I rubbed the sleep from my eyes to survey the near-darkness. What I saw, reflected in the oval mirror above the dresser, was the buoyant gloom alive and winking with sparks. A cloud of fireflies.

The wonder of it jolted me fully awake.

The clanging began again. Then it ceased.

For a moment, I forgot about the noise. Mother's soft breathing pulled at the silence, stealing away a bit of my nameless fear. As I shook Mah-ma to wake her so she could see the fireflies, there was a rush of wind. I turned my head to look at the windows. A strong breeze lifted the lace curtains and fluttered one of the three opaque pull-down shades. Pinpoints of outside light sprayed across the room and spangled gems across the ceiling. I looked back at the wide, tilted mirror, at the reflected lights dancing within. I remembered how fireflies came together to rescue lost children in the caves of Old China. Mah-ma, her back to me, mumbled something, then receded into sleep.

I sank into the bed and leaned tightly against Mah-ma's great warmth. The clanging grew louder. A monster was approaching. My mind conjured a wild, hairy creature, eyes like fire, heaving itself, and the chains it was dragging, towards our bedroom cave. I turned to stone.

My child's wisdom said that Mah-ma and I had to lie perfectly still, or the monster would veer towards our bed, open its hideous wet mouth and devour us. Rigidly, I watched the pinpoints of light crazily dancing up the wall and across the ceiling.

Suddenly the wind died.

The blind hung still, inert.

I looked up. A ceiling of stars shimmered above me. The monster would be dazzled by the stars. It would be fooled. It would turn away from us. We were sky, not earth. I shut my eyes and whispered, "Go away, monster! Go away!"

There was rattling and banging, a clinking, and then a crescendo of sharp, steady *clip-clop, clip-clops*....The monster, now frustrated by the lack of prey, shuddered—and turned into the milkman's old chestnut horse, its chains into *clink-clanking* bottles.

When I told Grandfather the next day how Mah-ma and I had escaped the hairy monster, he laughed. He said I was very smart to lie very still and not wake Mah-ma, who had been working two shifts and was tired. When I told Fifth Aunty, who often took care of me, she smiled, pinched my cheeks and said, "You lucky boy. Fireflies and stars always fortunate."

This haunting, Grandfather and Father both assured me, was only a child's dream. Many years later, Fifth Aunty reminded me of the old horse, how late one morning, when the milkman came to her alleyway door to sell her a strip of milk tickets, she had lifted me up to the animal's large, snorting head, and I, squirming in her arms, trembling, let it snatch a carrot stump from my palm.

"Only an old mare." She laughed.

Fifth Aunty told everyone how I had wiped the horse saliva on her face. I remembered none of it.

At five, I had my second haunting. This one, I recall clearly.

The distant clattering and clanging began again. I knew by now it was the sound of the approaching milkman. I lay still, listened for the comforting sound of the old horse, its hooves going *clip-clop, clip-clop* on the cobblestones, a rhythmic drumming that I can still hear today.

I sat up, not letting go of Mah-ma. She stirred and her breath deepened. My mother and I were utterly alone in the island kingdom of the double bed. Father was away again, on one of his frequent alternating three- and five-week stints as a cook on a Canadian Pacific steamship liner.

For my own amusement, I dared to imagine a slimy three-eyed monster somewhere in the dark outside, coming towards us, dragging its clanking chains.

I was lucky. I was brave. At will, I could render the great monster harmless and go back to sleep in the comfort of my own created magic. The chain's rattling had become as familiar as the sound of a chopstick hitting a milk bottle.

But that morning, for a reason I could not understand, I did not go back to sleep. From somewhere within me, a nameless fear slithered up my spine and gripped me by the nape of my neck. Then it began to pull me down. During the summer evening, the blanket and sheet had been pushed away. My pyjama top, rolled up, exposed my back. I could not reach the bedding wadded below my feet. I clung to Mah-ma, my cheek tight against her flannel nightgown. Her body heat and sweet salty smell anchored me.

As the morning sun began to bleach the darkness from the ceiling, the pinpoints of light faded. I needed to pee. But I did not get up and go down the hall, as I had been taught to do. An odd feeling fettered me, made me feel inadequate, like a helpless baby. And yet I knew that a big boy doesn't cry out for his *mah-ma*.

Carefully, I sat up.

A faint, distant clattering came through the open window: the milk wagon was lumbering down the street. I pushed myself off the big bed. The cold linoleum floor tickled my soles. I listened. The milk wagon halted. Except for Mother's breathing, and a scattering of birdsong, there was no sound. The world seemed to me to have suddenly altered, slipped into enchantment, like in a Grimm fairy tale.

In the near-dark, the scratched oak dressing table stood with squat authority. On its polished top lay a cluster of bottles filled with mysterious amber liquid, tortoiseshell combs, silver-topped jars, and fancy cylinders holding fragrant talc. I resolved to go there, pull out the seat, and climb up and play with the bottles. But then the single opened window dispatched a rapid tattoo of clopping hooves. The wind rose. The window shade lifted like a hand and beckoned me.

I was tall enough to lay my head on the window sill. Standing there, I then turned my head and stuck my tongue out to lick the rough, paint-flaked wood. It was real enough. I stared at the pull-cord ring swinging from the blind. When the wind faltered, the beige wooden ring *click-clicked* against the glass. Outside, the milkman's horse whinnied and shook its bells. The wagon stopped, started, stopped, started. My heart thumped against my chest. But I was not afraid of the milk wagon. It was something else I feared.

I turned my head and glimpsed, in the dresser mirror, my mother, a length of warm shadow stretched out along the far edge of the bed. From where I stood, I could not see the rise and fall of her back. Suddenly, I could not breathe: she seemed too still.

I swallowed hard and stared at her.

The milk wagon clattered on, the bump, bump, bump of the wheels on the cobblestones fading into nothingness. I did not cry out.

This is all I know of the second haunting.

To this day, the vision of that moment—me with my head on the window sill, breathless, watching my sleeping mother—has not left me. Whenever this image comes to me, unbidden, my heart pounds, my lungs constrict. I taste a second or two of panic, then, catching my breath, I tell myself I am being foolish.

Years after that moment, at the age of thirty-seven, I was at my mother's funeral, and Fifth Aunty was saying how pleased my mother must be that her last ride was in a *Cadillac*, and that Father had bought her such a fine oak casket.

"The lid good enough for a dining table, Sonny," she said, using my English name. "First class!"

Fifth Aunty leaned on my arm as we walked to my cousin's car. She looked up at the bright, cloudless sky and frowned. She had almost tempted the gods: if she made the funeral sound too perfect, the gods would humble us. She had to find something wrong. She stopped, casually curved her finger into her mouth and popped out her ill-fitting false teeth. They dropped into a Baggie. The handbag snapped shut. Fifth Aunty sighed; she was stalling, thinking how to tell me (as family should tell each other) what had gone wrong. She would have to be diplomatic, yet frank.

"Oh, but if you win the lottery, Sonny, you remember: I want a horse-drawn hearse. More fancy." She stopped, cleared her throat carefully. "Everything should take longer, Sonny. Cadillac so fast! Service too fast! Even your dear *mah-ma*, why so fast! Today everything too fast."

I laughed—exactly what Aunty wanted me to do. She went on, cheeks flapping. "If up to me, I order, you know, an *old* horse and a shining first-class wagon with lace curtains!"

Fifth Aunty touched my shoulder with her cane and giggled. Death never scared her. She had seen too much death in Old Chinatown. I told her that, if I won the big lottery, I would see her ride into the sunset in the grandest, and slowest, horse-drawn hearse.

"Remember that day you little boy and saw your very first one, Sonny?" she said. Aunty always went back to the old days.

"No, I don't," I said. "I remember big wagons."

"Yes, yes, you remember," she insisted. "We stand on Hastings Street, I hold your hand, and your aunty finally tell you that black thing no fancy milk wagon." Fifth Aunty broke into toothless laughter. "Oh, you looked so surprised that people died, just like your goldfish."

"What did I say?"

"You cry out, '*Mah-ma* won't *die!*'"

I think of that morning of the second haunting, when I was five years old—the haunting that has never left me. In my mind's eye, the looking glass reflects half the bed where my mother lies; its cool surface mirrors the dappled wall where my shadow first ambled towards the morning light.

As Fifth Aunty gets into the car, I know now why I stood there at the window, unable to speak. My cousin's car drives away.

I listen.

There is birdsong.

There is silence.

That early memory, that haunting, sends me on a search for other remembered moments. Some come in dreams, mere fragments, weighted with a sense of mystery and meaning. At such times, a sadness pervades me. I close my eyes: older, long-ago faces, a few of them barely smiling, push into my consciousness. I hear voices, a variety of Chinatown dialects, their singsong phrases warning me: "You never forget you Chinese!"

Now I am a child stumbling against Mother in an alley barely wide enough for two people, my three-year-old legs scooting two or three steps ahead of her. I am jerked backwards. "Walk properly," Mother says. I jump a few steps more, her arm extends and she tugs me back. I look up at the wintry strip of sky. We are going to visit someone who lives up the stairs at the back of the building.

"Remember what I told you to say," Mother cautions.

I nod, laughing.

"No"—her tone is solemn—"no *laughing*."

At the end of the narrow alley, Mother stops walking and kneels beside me. She wets her fingers and brushes down my cowlicks. Other people angle themselves to pass us. A damp wind whistles above us. Mother pulls me closer to her. A man wearing a black fedora pats my head and tells me I'm a good boy. Two women push by us. Each speaks a few words to Mother, and their long, dark coats brush against my face. Everyone is going in the same direction. Mother shakes me to get my attention.

"Whisper to me what you are going to say."

I whisper. Every word. Clearly.

"Good," Mother says, wetting her fingers to push back a lock of hair that has fallen over my eye. "Remember. No laughing."

We follow some people up the stairs to the second or third floor of the building. A long hallway holds cardboard boxes the size of me; the cartons are piled on top of each other against one wall. As Mother and I walk down the dim corridor, the two women in the dark coats, single-file ahead, look back at us, as if to make sure we are safely following them. I do not laugh. It does not feel like a place for laughing.

"She's in here," one of the women murmurs to Mother, and the two women step aside to let us through. Mother holds my hand as we enter a tiny room that smells of incense and medicine. On one side, a big woman bends over someone on a bed and whispers, "He's here."

Mother lifts me up. I see a lady with damp black hair straining to raise her head and focus her eyes on me. The pillow is embroidered with flowers. Mother says, "What do you have to say, Sonny?"

I gulp. I know what I have to say, but I can't understand why the lady does not ask me anything. I am not afraid, but what I was told to say sounds, to me, like an answer. And an answer needs a question. Finally, the lady on the bed smiles and nods at me. I am satisfied.

"I'm fine," I say. "My name is Choy Way Sun and I'm a good boy."

The lady on the bed breathes heavily and closes her eyes. Mother puts me down. Whatever was to be done is done. We walk out of the room and down the two or three flights of stairs, pushing against people coming the opposite way.

"My, my," a voice exclaims. There is whispering.

Mother says nothing, only pulls me along and back out onto Pender Street. I blink.

The street is filled with a bluish light.

Sexuality

ALWAYS CONTROVERSIAL, sexuality has recently drawn more attention with the realization that "sexualities"—gay, lesbian, straight, bi—is perhaps a better term to express the enactment of desire. This revised model has been responsible for a dazzling array of books and articles (not to mention films and videos) that represents those communities' diverse practices and that questions received notions of our sexual urges and how we express them. For Michel Foucault, one of the greatest late-twentieth-century thinkers, it's not so much that we're more liberated than earlier generations; it's that we've put our sexualities at the centre of the mystery of ourselves. Who we are, it appears, is, in this era, keyed to how we present ourselves sexually. The works that follow offer a small sampling of the wide-ranging sexualities acknowledged above.

STAN PERSKY,
excerpt

Autobiography of a Tattoo

Call Persky's contribution "queer travelling" if you like. *Autobiography of a Tattoo,* from which the following is taken, is an unabashed cruising of young men and different places with a little intellectualizing thrown in. Persky goes to Berlin for the summer (he also takes a few side trips). Mainly he desires and/or falls in love with a bunch of young guys. Interspersed with the "blow-by-blow" he tries to explain that desire and relate it to sexualities, gay and straight. The book, a kind of journal, contains a lot of material that seems to drift; however, it also offers a good, unguarded look at a "queer romantic," as it were.

Questions:

1. Is Persky convincing regarding pornography and its virtues? How does or doesn't he convince you?
2. How does Persky establish his conversational tone?
3. *Butler vs. the Queen*, a 1992 Supreme Court decision, is important to the Canadian political landscape and the regulation of pornography. Find and discuss it.
4. Do you think that it is easy to discuss porn in the logical way Persky does it?
5. What sources and tactics would you use to make your case on this issue?

My current favourite porn magazine consists of "still" photos from a sex video called *Folklore*. I bought the magazine last summer, and when I returned to Berlin this year and unpacked the little library I have here, I rediscovered and began studying it more carefully—if "studying" is the right word.

On the back cover is a photo of someone I've name "Dieter," sitting naked on a roughly hand-crafted chair in a barn (a ladder to the hayloft slants in front of him). Even in seated repose, his flat belly slack, pectoral muscles relaxed, left hand casually covering his genitals, he's a picture of "youth," a reminder of what goes as the middle-aged body sags.

There's an inset photo, on the same back cover, in which another young man I've named "Stefan," who looks enough like

Dieter to cause momentary confusion, stands bare-chested (pectoral muscles sharply defined), wearing a sports headband, elastic terrycloth wristbands, and a pair of pants decorated with coloured embroidery in a "folkloric" style (hence, I guess, the title of the film).

But for me, the point—or "punctum," as Roland Barthes in his book about photography, *Camera Lucida,* called that feature of a photo which stings your consciousness to attention—of the picture of the nude, seated Dieter, is the expression in his eyes and on his wide lips, and particularly the way he slightly tilts his head toward me (his hair is floppily parted in the middle). His look at once promises obedience to desire—his own, primarily, but perhaps not solely his own—and offers a hint of mischief, as if he'll ensure your obedience to his desire.

I'd seen him in a few previous photos in the magazine, engaged in sex with some of the other young men, including Stefan, whom I had immediately identified as the "hero" or erotic centre of the story, and wondered what Dieter's attitude was toward desire. (I'm almost, irrationally, tempted to say, "…what his attitude was toward *me.*") Feeling a tiny shock of illumination upon looking at his photo on the back cover (with its smile as faint as that of the Mona Lisa), I think, "Ah, so that's it," imagining I suddenly know something about his mind.

What are the enticements of that particular set of photos?

In looking at those images and contemplating descriptions of them, I'm entranced by the sense of potentially infinite, or at least exhaustive, descriptions, which fills me with the anticipation of pleasure in writing them, of describing Dieter, Stefan, and their friends in sexual play. Why do I imagine that to be such a pleasure?

It has something to do with language and eros being inextricably bound together for me—something to do with words and desire. I don't like wordless desire. I prefer articulations, admissions, confessions. Porn and much of erotic life present a mystifying silence. In a porn photo series, you're looking at various tableaux and have to figure out how the characters got from one situation to the next. Even in real sexual relations, the silence between people can result in one or both of the partners having no idea what the other thinks or feels.

During sex, people do the most extraordinary things in terms of acts, positions, desires, but if you say to them during or after some idiosyncratic act, "You want that, don't you?" or "You liked that, didn't you?", they often blush with embarrassment, can barely articulate a "yes." Language is what makes sex "human" for me, takes it beyond its necessarily (biologically-driven) "animal" aspects. In a sense, then, language rather than some particular act is what offers sexual "intimacy." When I imagine, with anticipatory pleasure, writing descriptions of *Folklore*, part of that pleasure is in speculating on the characters' motives, uttering their desires, redeeming the "inhumanity" of what's portrayed by imagining its articulation. Although all modes of porn can be enjoyable—writing, photos, videos, each has its attractive features for me—my preference for articulation explains why I somewhat prefer photos to video, and written descriptions to pictures.

Body note on "folk-porn": The title *Folklore* coincidentally reminds me that at about the time that homo porn videos began to become widely available through capitalist market production and distribution, in the early 1980s, a man in New York named Boyd McDonald began collecting and successfully publishing true accounts of homosexual experiences, encouraging people to tell their stories freely, irrespective of preconceptions of what might be acceptable—in short, to express their "perversity." McDonald argued that these often awkwardly written, amateur narratives (in effect, a genre of folk-porn) were frequently "better" and "hotter" than professional porn or art that encompassed sexual matter. Even before I encountered folk-porn, I'd noticed that the stories young men I slept with told me about their sexual experiences were more exciting than most other representations of sex. The collections that McDonald published (they had titles like *Meat, Flesh, Cum*) were indeed exciting precisely because they elicited revelations about desire that neither art nor commercial porn articulated.

Because thinking about homosexuality necessarily involves considering homo sex (that's why it's called homosexuality in the first place, right?)—which is itself inseparable from the problem of describing homo sex—pornography, as one model of representing homo sex, seems to me an inescapable consideration.

Since I grew up as an activist in the generation that created public homosexuality—at the time we called it, a bit grandiosely, "gay liberation"—before public representation of homo was widely available, the impact of pornography on us may have been considerably more powerful and lasting than for those who have been socialized with porn as an ordinary feature of homo milieux. At a time when the mere fact of homo sex was repressed and denied, homo porn served as a kind of documentary proof of homo's existence, as well as an instruction manual of sorts. Perhaps that's why I still find one of its functions to be the documentation of a resistance to the would-be suppression of representing homo desire.

In the presence of such a claim, someone will surely point out that since homo porn is a multibillion-dollar capitalist industry, there's virtually no resistance to it any more, except maybe from a few puritanical repressed homos who occupy various censorship offices. But that's not true, either literally or in terms of an analysis of contemporary global capitalism/tribalism. For example, the law of the land in Canada (the Canadian Supreme Court's 1992 *Butler v. the Queen* decision) upholds the country's obscenity law on the grounds that "degrading, demeaning, dehumanizing" porn is "degrading" whenever a substantial body of people "perceive" it to be such and that "degrading, demeaning," etc. porn causes legal "harm" because it gives men bad ideas which may lead to bad actions (I'm not making this up), and since Supreme Court decisions are very hard to rescind, this will remain the law for the foreseeable future or until Canada formally announces that it's taking early retirement as a nation-state. Since that decision, about the only porn that's been interdicted is homo porn.

Notwithstanding, one can argue that homo porn—as a product of the market—is widely available. I'm not ignoring that or how it affects the "meaning" of porn. But it's a mistake to think that the assimilation of porn by the market settles all the societal questions about it. Homo porn remains a matter of contention between the contending forces of society.

Capitalism has no objection to any profitable product, including homo-related ones, while tribalists (generally of the religious variety) oppose some kinds of capitalist products, particularly homo-related ones. Thus, the withering nation-state vacillates through phases of "liberalism" and "conservatism." At a societal level, today's resistance to homo porn increasingly takes the form of hostile "indifference." When it's articulated, it sounds like this: "I don't care what you fags do, just just keep your fucking hands off me and my kids." Which is to say that a lot of people are opposed to imaginings of homo sex either in their own minds or in the world. Since the workings of capitalism and its seeming alliance with liberalism (read: "fucking fags") are not transparent to such people, they are puzzled when their bosses restrain them from shutting up fags. Which then leads to privatized "gay-bashing."

More important than whether my estimate of opposition to homo porn is mere nostalgia, is the question of "degrading, demeaning," etc. And this, I suspect, requires some consideration of pornography in general. *Folklore* isn't degrading *unless* one thinks (as some feminists do about heterosexual porn) that porn is *by definition* rather than by content degrading. If you don't think that porn is degrading by definition, then you have to look at content—and by content, I mean social/political/historical circumstances as well as particular acts. Here we're not talking about, in terms of critical categories, such things as "silly" or "boring," we're talking about the more debatable notion of "degrading."

If someone in a porno performance says, "Oh baby, I really wanna suck your big beautiful dick," is that degrading? If that utterance occurs in a homo representation like *Folklore*, the answer is no. If that's said by a woman in a het porno, someone could argue that the gender "politics" of the situation render the statement degrading. They're welcome to argue the case, but I think it's going to be difficult to sustain.

It seems to me that a lot of the arguments made in debates about porn in recent years have been of the "by definition" variety, or that definitions of content are extended to the point that it amounts to the same thing as "by definition." For example, take one of the standard objections to hetero porn—that it "objectifies" women. Whatever you think of that objection, it doesn't apply to homo porn in the same way, for a very simple reason. In hetero porn, the notion of objectification is dependent on a male viewer (and producer) looking at women as objects. But in homo porn, the viewer not only sees the young men as others (or objects) but also identifies with them as subjects, often shifting back and forth in imagination with any number of those represented. The homo viewer may imagine he's doing the fucking or is the recipient of it. In any case, in homo porn of the *Folklore* kind, which is representative of the overwhelming majority of homo porn, there simply isn't any violence, coercion, rape, or whatever else might provide substantive grounds for seeing it as demeaning. In *Folklore* there's just, as the advertising text claims, a lot of randy young men (or young men who have agreed to act randy).

A more sophisticated case is made by serious critics of the distortions of reality. They agree that the current formal objections to porn are arguable at best. The real objections, they say, are that the sexuality represented is fake, that it miseducates (people don't really fuck like that, the configurations are all designed to enable camera intrusion), that it's artistically beyond being bad, and that the pleasure is simulated.

I restrict myself here to homo porn because that's what I know something about, and because the objections to porn in general (which I'm not pretending to be cloddishly unaware of) involve a more extended political argument than can be made in this context. I'm persuaded, however, that *if* there's an argument to be made against hetero porn, it won't apply equally to homo porn, unless one makes the case with a degree of philosophical depth that suggests there's simply something wrong with the whole idea of getting actual people to engage in sex for other people's viewing. Certainly, this is a conceivable argument, but I've yet to hear a persuasive version of it.

With respect to "realist" objections: at one level, homo porn, in addition to whatever else it is, is a documentation of something that took place in the world. The pleasure may be simulated, the sex isn't unless, again, you import a "by definition" notion of what counts as sex. That the represented relations are fictionalized doesn't undercut the fact that person x and person y did act z. Nor is the documentary character of it vitiated by the fact that the document is edited for marketing purposes.

The homo sex in *Folklore* looks to me like a fairly realistic representation of homo sex. Sure, homo porn idealizes, and thereby distorts homo sex—that is, it makes it seem better than it is, the people in it are prettier than real life, it leaves sexual failure on the cutting-room floor, etc.—but the viewer knows that. The problem-free orgiastic romps are fantasy, sure, but the representations of acts of sex aren't; the sociology is magic realism, the fucking journalism. Insofar as it's "educational," I don't see that it fails as "vocational training."

Naturally, it's organized so that a camera can film it—it is, after all, a film—but to claim that the configurations are all designed to enable camera "intrusion" seems neither entirely true nor relevant. There are some changes from "real" sex for filmic purposes (pulling out before ejaculating, for example), but the viewer knows about that, too, and isn't being essentially fooled.

As for aesthetic judgments, the natural comparison isn't art but television. Porn seems to me at least as good as most television—I find it aesthetically preferable to t.v. and comparable in its aesthetic goals. Those who think that the comparison to television is trivial (i.e., that it takes t.v. too seriously), strike me as being snobbish about television. Or if they're devotees of t.v. and think that the comparison is trivial because it takes porn too seriously, then it seems to me they're being snobs about porn. As for the simulation of pleasure, even there one oughtn't be too hasty, given the diversity of human desire. Sometimes one notices in looking at porn that the performers seem to be "really into it." Naturally, it's hard to do sex in front of cameras, hard to keep cocks hard, hard to "get into it," and expectedly, there's some "fluffing" of cocks off-camera. If the "realist" objection is that the young men have been assembled and paid to do it, and that no lasting relationships will be formed as a result, well—really.

When there were few representations of homo sex available (say prior to 1970), almost any description of it in literature, even the crudest pulp ones, had a certain interest. Lately, and this is no doubt a response to the commercial availability of it, I've become more circumspect about sexual representation: writing about sex, the literal details often seem obsessive, an expression of vanity, an intrusion on everyone's privacy, including the reader's. Anyway, by now it's been done to death. Now, I'll insist on a literal detail only when it's relevant to the story; I become more interested in Psyche, in the "psychology" of a sex act, than in enumerating the orifices in which it occurred, and describing the entrances and exits.

MARGARET DRAGU AND A.S.A. HARRISON,
excerpt

Revelations: Essays on Striptease and Sexuality

Revelations: Essays on Striptease and Sexuality, published in 1988, mixes confessional moments—mostly Margaret Dragu's about her time as a stripper—with social and political commentary by A.S.A. Harrison. The tone is carnal, even jokey; note, for instance, some of the chapter titles: "Why Queen Elizabeth Doesn't Strip" and "Getting Down with the Boys." The book reveals that both authors are clearly comfortable with the topic and their involvement with stripping. There is little, if any, moralizing here; indeed, the hostility to stripping they mention is generally seen to be symptomatic of sexual repression. *Revelations* attempts, also, to play it fair—both male and female stripping are investigated.

Questions:

1. Harrison's opening paragraphs are "classical"—clear and concise, with the thesis presented lucidly. Discuss this tactic.
2. The italicized sections are meant to work differently than the main body of the text. How and why?
3. "We have come to believe that sexual thrills lie in the realm of the forbidden." Is this true?
4. Harrison's work shows less strain than Fawcett's. Do you agree with this statement? Compare the strengths of the two excerpts.
5. How does Harrison work women's issues into her piece?

We live in a culture where any expression of sexuality outside of adult heterosexual mating is, in some sense, a problem. Homosexuality, prostitution, incest, adultery, stripping, pornography—most everyone would experience some relief if these things went away. Our sexual code of ethics is rigid and exclusive. Its foundation is the centuries-old belief that sex is wrong and dangerous, and must therefore be closely regulated.

This belief is a part of our sexual history and culture. We are so closely allied with it that it is all but invisible to us. We don't see it as a belief at all, but rather understand it to be truth and reality. "Look what the stripper is doing," we say. "That's disgusting." We fail to notice that it is nothing more than the belief itself that horrifies us as we project it onto various sexual activities.

Strippers and other sexual workers put themselves on the line, not because of their sexual choices per se, but because, in this society, sexual offenders of any kind are outcasts. Our contempt for strippers has the same basis as our contempt for rapists. We condemn those who break the sexual code—at whatever level.

There are particular rules against sexuality in women. Only a hundred years ago, sexual desire in women was actually considered to be an illness, for which doctors prescribed treatments such as hot douches and blood letting. Today, we continue to mistrust sexually expressive women.

The low status of stripping is implicit in our sexual code. Stripping can only live down to its reputation, and thus obligingly reinforce our belief that it is an unwholesome activity. As we point the finger, we seem to be unaware that we are lost in a game of moral tail-chasing. Our views construct the parameters within which sexual entertainment must exist.

One way out of this dilemma is to consider strippers in their role of conscientious objector. From a historical perspective, strippers can be seen as women who are in active revolt against the dictate that their sexuality is shameful. A stripper may or may not have developed a political ideology around her work, but every stripper is aware that she is defying the sexual code, and many strippers have an instinctive understanding of the social implications of doing just that.

Historically, the taboos around women's bodies and sexuality have helped to create and maintain the low status of women. The device of women's clothing is an example of how this works. It is not very difficult to imagine the repressive physical and psychological effects of wearing many of the garments designed for women in the 19th century. For example, there were poke bonnets, which eliminated peripheral vision; tightly-laced corsets, which enforced shallow breathing and were painful besides, and sometimes caused deformation and even death; boned bodices, which kept women upright; as many as fourteen layers of petticoats, which made for considerable bulk and weight; metal-cage crinolines; steel or wire bustles; drop shoulders, which restricted arm movements; tied-back skirts known as the single trouser, which made walking difficult and running impossible; and finally trailing trains and abundant drapings and flounces, which made it necessary to move about with extreme caution.

Women's clothing was designed to cover the body almost completely, and in many cases it created a formal, stylized body shape, which served to distort and thereby hide the body's natural contours. The fashions described were accepted, in their time, as decent and respectable dress for women. To rebel could only invite social ostracism. At the same time, such clothing literally dictated repression, for to live in perpetual physical discomfort makes it difficult to move, and almost impossible to think.

What is interesting here is that the rules for covering, disguising and inhibiting the body were based in the belief that women's bodies are shameful. In other words, the bias against women's sexuality has been a major device for keeping women out of the world. So many of the rules of conduct that apply only to women spring from this bias. Real equality for women can only come with the acceptance of women's sexuality, and the release of all taboos associated with it.

Sexual equality would mean a lot for women, but it would have vast implications for society as a whole. For example, prostitution would probably disappear, or if it did not disappear, then it would be shared as a profession by men and women alike. If female worth no longer rested on chastity, then women's bodies would not be in any greater demand than men's as sexual objects. Also, because there would be no particular stigma attached to women's sexual activities, the attitude of contempt towards women in sexual contexts would evaporate. The school of pornography that depicts the sexual abuse of women would no longer have any social basis or meaning.

If we did have sexual equality, then sex in general would probably enjoy much greater acceptance, since it is women who carry the sexual taint. People would be able to enjoy sex at more levels and in more contexts. If we did not repress our sexual feelings they would not become distorted by guilt, and perverse sexual attitudes would have no context in which to flourish. Sexual entertainment would evolve and improve, and would become more meaningful for both men and women. All of this is simply to say that sexual repression in general, and particularly the repression of women's sexuality, is at the base of our sexual distress as a society.

Women have gained a lot of sexual freedom over the past hundred years. Some of the credit for this must go to sexual entertainers, for it is impossible to make this kind of gain without women who are willing to work on the cutting edge of sexual change. This can be seen more clearly in a historical context.

For example, during the late 19th century, women's legs became a strong focus for moral outrage. It was a time when even the mention of women's legs was considered to be shocking and indecent. The word *limb,* and the French word *jambe* were used as euphemisms. Women's legs were of course completely covered and disguised by voluminous skirts that generally touched the ground. The so-called short skirt that came and went during the period never fell shorter than ankle length.

The general infamy associated with women's legs is brought home by the story of a gift of silk stockings that was offered to a Spanish queen on the occasion of her marriage. The stockings were refused with the rebuke: "The Queen of Spain has no legs."

In defiance of this trend, women entertainers in New York, Paris, and London began showing their legs in the theatre. The thing was to wear tights, and thus reveal the clearly delineated form of the leg without going so far as to actually expose the flesh. The most daring displays featured tights that were flesh-coloured to simulate nudity.

The uproar these shows caused can hardly be believed. An actress of the period said that every time she revealed her tights-clad leg through the slit in her skirt, it was greeted by great guffaws from some of the men present. Meanwhile, ministers, politicians, suffragettes, and other morally-minded people organized campaigns and demonstrations in attempts to stop the outbreak of so-called nudity and vice.

The battle continued for many decades, and then, towards the end of the century, women's fashions began to change. In

1895, bloomers worn with thick stockings became a popular cycling costume for women. The bloomers of the time were so voluminous that they served, like skirts, to disguise the form, but they ended just below the knee, and so revealed the shape of the calf and ankle. This costume scandalized a great many people, and some bloomer wearers even had stones thrown at them, but the more daring continued to wear them.

In the final decade of the 19th century, skirts began to narrow at the ankles, coming dangerously close to acknowledging the existence of the lower leg. It was soon after this that the slit skirt came into being. Here was a fashion that finally admitted the lower leg into society, for slit skirts were worn at fashionable gatherings and with transparent stockings. From here, it was an easy slide into the 1920s, when women were wearing their skirts to mid calf. It should be mentioned that it was only with this initial acknowledgement of women's legs that it became plausible for women to wear trousers.

The movement continued to its logical conclusion, culminating with the miniskirt of the 1960s, and the total acceptance of pants and shorts as street wear for women. The result is that women's legs have been completely destigmatized. As far as legs go, women have gained equality with men.

This one breakthrough, which took a hundred years to achieve, has revolutionized the lives of women. The physical advantages range from suntanning to free movement. On a professional level, the change has allowed women to make a place for themselves in sports and jobs that were formerly open only to men. The purely psychological benefits are unknowable, but undoubtedly great.

It is impossible to say how much the leg revolution was helped along by the women entertainers who began by showing their legs in the theatre. The First World War did a lot to bring in practical and comfortable clothing for women. But considering the hysteria that greeted the first exhibitions of women's legs in the 1860s, it was probably vital to do some initial work in the formal and relatively safe arena of the theatre.

SEXUALITY

Many Victorian sexual taboos appear ridiculous from our present perspective of relative emancipation. We can now laugh at things like bathing machines, which provided women (men did not use them) with curtained steps so that they could descend into the ocean without being seen, in the interests of modesty, even though they were absurdly overdressed for swimming by our standards. And yet, the way we think about sex today is essentially no different from the way the Victorians thought about sex. We are more liberal, but we are quite as self-righteous and single-minded when it comes to our sensitive areas.

Strippers and other sexual entertainers undertake the job of pushing on our sexual limits in one way or another—by testing them, defying them, or even just exposing them. Sexual entertainment in the theatre provides an interesting cultural exposition, and because it informs the leading edge of sexual propriety, one of the things it can show us is where we are heading in terms of our sexual evolution. With this in mind, it is very telling that female strippers are becoming a thing of the past in some of the larger, more permissive western cities such as Berlin and New York. The progressive trend is to trim sex shows down to exclusively physical values. This doesn't quite come off in the striptease context, and is evidently confusing and demoralizing for the few strippers that persist in the midst of these values. As an example, here is Dragu's description of her visit to a New York strip club.

> *The Melody Berlesk was in the 42nd Street zone. A sign outside proclaimed that "berlesk" still lived there. My friend and I walked up the stairs to an old-fashioned theatre, similar to Le Strip here in Toronto, with rows of seats, a runway stage, and no booze. It was about six bucks admission. Elevator muzak was playing as we took our seats. There were five other people in the audience—none of them sitting together.*
>
> *A voice introduced the first stripper, and a girl left the dressing room and walked up the stairs to the stage. The first one was so forgettable I can't remember a thing about her. The second stripper was a black girl—*

quite elegant in old-fashioned stiletto heels and a few pieces of lilac chiffon and a g-string. She had a nice presence and strutted well. She quickly whipped off all her clothes, including her g-string, sat on a chair in the middle of the runway, and did a long spread show. She had good form—pointed her toes and was smooth as butter—but she was very distant and disinterested. After her act, which closed with a faint smattering of applause, there was more muzak and a five-minute wait.

The third stripper came out—an energetic, chunky blonde in a sparkly aquamarine costume of bra, panties and g-string, all matching and very off-the-rack. She actually danced to the muzak! She was in her mid thirties and had a pot belly. Her smile glittered like fake jewels, and her eyes were hard.

She took it all off lickety-split, including the g-string, lay down on the runway, and got down to some heavy tit rubbing and a split beaver presentation to the bald guy sitting front-row centre. She spent a good ten minutes on her back, wiggling around and moaning and laughing and rubbing and receiving a steady flow of one-dollar bills from the bald guy. He never smiled once—just continued to shell out the bills. She milked him and milked him, like a porno-puppet cash register.

At one point her music stopped dead mid song—some kind of technical problem. She just sat up on the stage letting her belly hang out and started to count her money. One of the guys a few rows over called out to her in the silence, asking if she was mad about the music stopping, and she answered, "Nah, as long as I'm getting tipped I don't give a fuck."

She sat like a greedy four-year-old with candy, mesmerized by her money and counting and recounting it until the music started again.

This time it was even more dreadful wallpaper-type muzak—show hits from old Broadway productions done in saccharine arrangements of a thousand and one strings from elevator land. Truly horrible. She wiggled down onto her back and finished milking the unsmiling old bald guy until the song was over, then collected the rest of her money and her clothes and split.

The most recent formal innovation in sex entertainment is the private booth, where patrons can watch coin-operated video on small screens; or look at live shows through peepholes that have coin-operated shutters. Some of the booths provide for a degree of contact with a sex performer in an adjacent booth. The private booth allows a patron to select a specific product, and to interact privately with that product. It also allows him to make a minimal commitment to the product, since each dollar buys only a few minutes. Thus, sex is neatly commodified for individual consumption.

Meanwhile, the content of sex shows is becoming more explicit on a purely physical basis. Pornographic video makes no attempt to introduce emotion, atmosphere, romance, intelligence, or any value other than that of physical explicitness. Currently popular are closeups of the sexual organs and juices of man, woman and beast; interminable views of sexual poking, rubbing, pumping and sucking; and sometimes representations of physical abuse. It is fascinating that we have come to a point where this is what we produce and consume as sexual entertainment, and in many ways it seems appropriate.

We have always focused our suppression of sex on its purely physical aspects, and so it is natural that we also pursue sexual revelation at the physical level. We have projected our desire (as well as our guilt) onto the physical body, particularly the female body, and have proceeded to strip it bare in order to interact with our desire. This a perfectly valid process, and one that has served us well for a long time, but we seem to be reaching the end of the line. At one time, a passing glimpse of a woman's ankle could make a man feel faint with excitement. Today, even a good long look at a woman's inner labia is losing its charge.

We have revealed that which was forbidden to be revealed, and made it accessible to almost anyone who wants it. The exposé is nearing completion, and the vital question is: where do we go from here? If we stay within our present system of values, all we can really do is to continue along the same lines, and since we have about covered the common ground, that means we must create representations of more novel, exclusive and fetishistic sexual acts.

In this way, we are making a gradual shift in focus, and this shift is a real turning point in our sexual culture. The form is outreaching its social function, which has so far been to challenge and expose the repressive rules of the existing sexual code. We are now beginning to make sexual entertainment that has no basis in our commonality, and therefore in most cases, no basis in our actual desire. We have come to believe that sexual thrills lie in the realm of the forbidden, so we must seek out whatever remains forbidden and go there.

Sexual entertainment may be moving into decadence, but there is no point in blaming it for our problems. The underlying issue is our massive sexual dissatisfaction as a culture. No matter how far we go into the sexually explicit or bizarre, still it is not enough. For a century, we strove to uncover the female body, and when this finally happened it did not bring fulfilment. We have not found the sexual entertainment that enables us to sit back and say: "This is good. This is satisfying." We have learned to equate fulfilment with novelty, and within that equation satisfaction is impossible.

In New York's modern sex emporiums, one senses a growing hysteria at our inability to make sexual representations that are deeply satisfying. The sexual entertainment available there is like fast food. We may crave it, and keep going back for more, and even exist on a steady diet of it, but it is not enough. We are complex beings, with many different kinds of needs. Sexuality is complex, and exists as an emotional, intellectual and spiritual need as well as a physical one.

We are caught in a moral loop that involves the alternating repression and expression of physical acts of sex. So focused are we on this fascinating dichotomy that we fail to see a universe out there.

SEXUALITY

KAREN/MIRANDA AUGUSTINE,

"bizarre women, exotic bodies & outrageous sex: or if annie sprinkle was a black ho she wouldn't be all that"

From the title to the conclusion, this is a hard-hitting, polemical essay. It is saturated with the politics of sexuality. For karen/miranda augustine, the seemingly progressive "lezzie" scene contains vestiges of racism. This launches her angry, forthright engagement with the current and past sexualization, particularly of Black women but also of Black men. augustine unapologetically identifies herself as "a consumer of pornography." She is not, however, as her article shows, an unaware consumer. Her catalogue of racial stereotypes in porn and erotica reveals a strong resistance to a racism that lingers in the most surprising places.

Questions:

1. Why do you think the author signs herself karen/miranda augustine?
2. How in such a short article does augustine scrutinize issues of race and sexuality?
3. Sarah Bartmann, the "Hottentot Venus," is cited as an historical example of racism and sexuality. Discuss the impact of this example.
4. The densely worded question that closes the essay is a vital one for augustine. Does it, despite its complexity, reverberate with possibilities?
5. Does this essay or others in this reader test the boundaries of the "proper" essay for you?

The new school of lezzie pro-sex activism has been pushed into the mainstream of queer political thought. Important as it is for women's issues to be placed at the centre, and particularly so since lesbians generally have little emotional or financial dependence on men, throughout the bulk of sex mags, porn, and the Modern Primitives trend, at heart is an unacknowledged presence of culture-vulturism dependent on racialized sex-drives of white queers.

As a queer-identified Black woman, I have felt unsatisfied by the sexual liberation rhetoric firmly anchored within lesbian and gay spaces. S/M, dyke representation, censorship, pornography, sexual fantasies: this cornucopia of women's sexual practice within the mainstream of the lesbian, gay and bisexual communities has conveniently disregarded the very complex issue of race—and where it all fits—within these discussions.

I'm not big on sexuality theories because the very things that swell my clit, when thrown into the whirlwind of lezzie political correctness, just don't figure. And depending on how strong I'm feeling, shame is often the outcome if what's turning me on is deemed degrading to my sex by the progressive elite. Put quite simply, I don't claim definitive politics on a lot of these issues, but I do understand what makes me wet.

I am a consumer of pornography. Het porn, that is. I have been so since the age of 11. *Cherie, Penthouse*...you name it, I hoarded it. What I realized then was that Black female porn stars (like their Asian, Latina, Arab and Jewish sisters) were left to the pages of fetish mags, alluding to themes of cannibalism, bestiality and slavery. What I understand now is that race is the distinguishing feature in determining the type of objectification a woman will encounter. And believe me, the sex libbers of the queer scene need a wake-up call: this problem is alive and well and deeply embedded within our communities. This in mind, a historical briefing on Black sexual exoticization will bring me back to my case in point.

the 411

Links made between the eroticization of Black sexuality, myths surrounding "whiteness" and colonial culture are lacking in the bulk of queer sex-lib theories. In examining the supposed normality of "whiteness" and the colonial construction of Black sexuality—and more importantly, how to reconceptualize that image—a different impression of the interconnectedness of race, class, gender, sexuality, power and control would emerge.

The use of Black women's bodies as fetish and "entertainment" for Europeans has its roots within the colonization of Africa. In France during the 18th and 19th centuries, the sexuality of African slaves was studied by scientists, naturalists and writers. The results deemed the African woman as primitive and therefore more sexually intensive. Interestingly enough, these "studies" which separated the African/"them" from the European/"us"— not just physically, but morally—distorted African sexual agency, and pathologized women's sexuality on the whole. The cult of (white) womanhood was confined to notions of purity, chastity, passivity and prudence. Black womanhood was polarized against white womanhood in the structure of the metaphoric system of female sexuality—the Black woman became closely identified with illicit sex.

Sarah Bartmann's girlie show

The genitalia of selected African slave women—referred to as "Hottentots"—was examined in order to prove them a primitive species who most likely copulated with apes. According to Sander Gilman, Sarah Bartmann, one of many African women placed on display and referred to as the "Hottentot Venus," is but one example of Black female objectification during early 19th century Europe. Her display formed one of the original icons for Black female sexuality; Bartmann was often exhibited at fashionable parties in Paris, generally wearing little clothing, to provide entertainment. To her audience, she represented deviant sexuality. Reduced to her sexual parts, Ms. Bartmann was showcased for about 5 years until her death at age 25 in 1815. To add insult to injury, her genitalia were dissected and, until recently, put on display at the Musée de l'Homme in Paris.

Present day notions of "freed" and "open" sexuality rely on this historically-specific interpretation of Black womanhood.

fuck lea delaria & her big black dildo jokes

question: which is more intimidating? a) a man, b) a big man, c) a big black man? question: rough sex—who are you most likely to get it from? a) an Asian, b) an African? question: what makes Latinos so "hot-blooded"?

The onslaught of dyke sex paraphernalia, in an attempt to overthrow the strictures of (white) womanhood, reinserts itself by commodifying "otherness" within certain sexual/body practices:

- body piercing, tattoos and scarification are a part of the Modern Primitives (an offensive and loaded term) movement, forms of body adornment inherent within Indigenous and Eastern cultures;
- in *Leatherwomen*, a book of women's sex writings, a (straight-identified) white woman is gang raped by 1 Black and 2 Latina women (never mind that Blacks, Latinos and First Nations form the majority of those incarcerated) who are portrayed as being sexually "deviant" and violent;
- and, in *Love Bites*, a book of lez-sex photography, white dykes fuck each other with big, black dildos.

Talks regarding the representation of women in porn and erotic writings have for too long privileged white gender and sexuality. Unchallenged racism is reflected in both het and queer smut: Black men are reduced to the size and effectiveness of their penises, while Black, Asian, Latina, Arab and Jewish women are viewed as anomalies, exotic treats and fetishes. Stereotypical notions of a person-of-colour's body suggest intense sexual pleasure unknown to the vanilla experience.

cross-over vanillas

Reactionaries from the queer-cracker league may claim censorship over my blatant observations of race and representation. And reactionaries from the pink third space may attempt to regulate how we, as queers-of-colour, should knock boots proper (read: no S/M).

Yet most needed is a level of acknowledgement and social understanding regarding the cultural specificities of sexual expression. Non-sexual examples include how dancehall, rap and Black speech are misinterpreted in the mainstream by non-Black audiences. And how, in porn and other sex-smut, the racialization of Black and Brown people is taken to the nth power and most extreme level. Perhaps what I'm trying to express most is that a lot of the debates presume that we are all white and that the confines of white body culture apply to us all. And this just isn't so.

Stressed here is not a simple trashing of lezzie-fuck culture, but the limitations and myopia of a sex-lib scene that is stuck in the rut of racial ambivalence. What one has the right to fantasize about or sexually express is not the issue here. The question *How entrenched is that sexual fantasy/practice in the myth of progressive representation and the transcendence of white patriarchal expression?* is key.

Media

THE LEADING GURU of contemporary culture, Jean Baudrillard, distinguishes our era from those before it by the proliferation of media. For him, and for many other thinkers, much that we do and learn is media-fed and mediated; that is, cameras record our acts to the point that we feel our lives are validated only when they are represented by media. City-TV, in Toronto, sends its reporters out to cover the city with a video camera. When those reporters sign off from the crime scene—or wherever they are situated—another camera captures them in turn, holding their cameras. Our behaviour, therefore, has changed. One example involves the whole public/private split; nowadays, most outrageously on shows like *Jerry Springer*, we seem to want to perform our "secret" selves—have them acknowledged. This leads Baudrillard to the conclusion that our realities are simulacral; that is, as much simulated or composed of images as they are real. Not that this state of affairs is bad by any means—websites broadcasting from the perspective of anti-globalization protesters gave a far different version of events in Seattle or Quebec City than more conservative mainstream media did.

CHANGING IDENTITIES

DANIEL RICHLER,

"Books on T.V."

Daniel Richler once hosted a book show on TVOntario, Ontario's English public television channel—hardly a show or a venue with the makings of "smash hit" written on it. Nonetheless, while its ratings didn't register on the same scale, say, as *The Sopranos*, the show *Imprint* did create a minor sensation. People who didn't read or write for a living actually watched it. That it was Richler's mixture of hipness and intelligence that boosted the ratings quickly became evident when, once he stopped hosting the show, the ratings plummeted. In addition to "doing" T.V., Richler is also a writer of some repute. Here, he provides the introduction to a book of interviews with writers.

Questions:

1. Richler's ability to mix literature and other media is evident here. How does he do it?
2. Much of this essay is anecdotal. Is this a good strategy for a seemingly dry topic?
3. Note the linkage of Burt Reynolds and Robertson Davies—pop culture "meets" high art. Is this juxtaposition another useful tactic?
4. There's one more example of juxtaposition: "putz" and "micturate." How does Richler's diction contribute to "Books on T.V."?
5. What national stereotypes are played on here?

In 1989, TVOntario commissioned me to investigate how a book show might fly in Canada. So I phoned around. I asked several authors how they felt about being on the box. The early results of this poll told me that TV appearances are more taxing for writers than for ordinary people.

Martin Amis said he'd always hated it: "It's the fear of disgracing yourself. I used to want to smoke to calm my nerves, but I'd end up pinching the cigarette between my knees because I didn't dare hold up my shaking hands in front of the camera. Then one day my interviewer said, 'Excuse me, Mr. Amis, for interrupting, but your trousers are on fire.'"

Ian McEwan revealed, with characteristic spleen, "I always feel a pot of tea is half-way down my cock."

John Irving recalled for me his time on the *Dick Cavett Show*. Cavett's reliance on research cards for questions and factoids so enraged him, he demanded whether the host had read his book. Well, no, said Cavett, actually, not yet. Irving walked off the set. "If the ignorant pretentious prick had admitted to it before the show began," he told me, "I would have understood—you can't be expected to read everything—but putting on that blithe, sophisticated act of his really made me want to puke."

Getting books on the air, not to mention their authors, was going to be rough.

I happened to be holidaying in Europe that summer and looked up Bernard Pivot. His world-famous program, *Apostrophes*, was in its second decade and so successful it commanded a special "Books of the week" table in virtually every bookstore in France; it was accessible in quiz and encyclopedia form on the country's Minitel database network; and it fuelled a European literary magazine called *Lire*. Its enduring success at home, meanwhile—on La Chaine (TVOntario's French-language sister station)—was a tweak on the noses of Canadians who professed to have a literary culture of their own. Yes, I presented myself as an innocent holiday maker but was in fact on a poaching mission.

Apostrophes' format was not complicated: before a live audience, six authors gathered to chat. The themes they were asked to explore were not infrequently saucy: "Sexy, les Seins," "Pudeur, Impudeur" and "Ca va Saigner." I might have overlooked this fact, were it not for the cover *of Lire* the week I was in Paris. It displayed

89

a nude woman reading in bed, its main feature erotic literature. Laurence Kaufmann, Antenne 2's PR person, assured me rather sternly that whatever I was suggesting, all this pointed to was a mere coincidence, but I had stopped listening; by then my mind was on fire. I pictured Robertson Davies in a pose recalling Burt Reynolds, a typewriter, hot from recent use, strategically placed.

Anyway, it might have been the jet lag, but having taken our seats in the studio for Pivot & Co.'s round table on the secrets of the Romanovs' cuisine, or some such arcana, my wife fell asleep on my shoulder—and this was her first appearance on French national television. For, unimpeachably intelligent though the show may have been, *Apostrophes* did not always deliver the high jolt-a-minute quotient that would be crucial to success on Canadian TV. I suspected that some of *Apostrophes'* reputation around the world rested *un peu trop* on one notorious episode from some eight years earlier, in the middle of which Charles Bukowski, drunk and bellicose, had been hauled off the set.

At the post-taping cocktail party, I asked Pivot if in his estimation an *Apostrophes*-type show could be reproduced elsewhere. Modestly he replied, "Oh *mais oui*. Anyone could do it." Then he thought about his own remark for a moment and added, "You know, Sweden tried and failed—they're such a cold people, I suppose that's why. And Belgium tried it, but it went nowhere. They're so...plain, it was inevitable. And the Italians, *alors*, on every show within fifteen minutes they'd be at one another's throats, so they took it off the air. So no, no—I would say it is not so possible."

I thought about North America, a continent with more guns than books on her subways; where schools prioritize conflict resolution courses over spelling; where mail goes undelivered while disgruntled postal workers roam the inner cities. Given the viciousness of literary criticism in our neck of the woods, I'd want a weapons check before each interview.

Speaking of America, at that time even the Book Of The Month Club with its 1.7 million members and over thirty participating television stations had failed to make a book show fly.

When I asked BOMC president Al Silverman what he'd do differently were he given another go, he despondently suggested, "Install a better-stocked bar?"

It's to TVOntario's great credit, then (in particular English Programming Head Don Duprey and then-Chairman Bernard Ostry), that against all the odds a book show was launched.

Arguably more than other shows, *Imprint* faced a challenge to please every variety of viewer, every type of reader. We felt, for example, that we bore some responsibility to nurture young readers, and so we featured the occasional punk descant and the occasional punk. I remember *Maggotzine #3*, which featured: "Mondo Sexo-rama zinetime; shrunken heads, robot orchestras, grasshopper wrestling, pussy pussy, self-mortification and more." Some fans of Alice Munro were not thrilled by the editor, a mohawked subterranean with an ice-tong in her nose. Conversely, we were not able to avoid "Modernity and Its Discontents—The Death of the Prairie Novel?" forever. And when we did, I just know we got zapped.

We fired away regardless, with both barrels: on the one hand punctuating the show with videos and film clips, sales charts and reading lists, dramatizations, contests, viewer mail, news hits and comedy skits; on the other, simply cramming the hour with every kind of writer we could find. Wags say if Shakespeare were alive today, he'd be writing sitcoms. Well, we're not snobs. He'd still get on the show. Chinese dissident poets, gangsta rappers, Tolkien freaks, gay pornographers, the toeheads who write the so-called instruction you get with your VCR, even political speech writers, all are welcome.

I have to say that without the existence of Toronto's Harbourfront Authors' Festival (run by the formidable Greg Gatenby) we would have had a relatively impoverished program. It would have been too expensive for us to fly all those authors in, whereas half the time we gorged for free at the trough and came up with, week after week, faces from all over: Michael Holroyd, Hanan Al-Shaykh, Ngugi wa Thiongo, Rian Malan, William Golding, Bapsi Sidhwa, Caryl Phillips....In this way, the innumerable Canadian authors we brought on the show were seen to share the world stage; that is as many of them really do, of course, but it is a perception that needs to be reinforced often, for Canadian audiences to appreciate the value of their own artists.

Serendipitously, *Imprint* also stumbled into the cleansing fire of political correctness, making for some white-hot arguments and lending the show an urgent, newsy flavour. Debate over racism in publishing, sexism in novels, and ageism in lullabies may well have struck some viewers as overwrought, but the point is that it struck a lot of viewers, one way or another, and reinforced what lovers of literature have always known (as Ezra Pound put it, so succinctly that we put it on our T-shirts): Literature is news that *stays* news.

As this book is published, *Imprint* enters its sixth year on the air, hosted now by the gumptious Guy Lawson. It has earned its place as an established forum where thoughtful people may express themselves at length. It is frequently raw, rude, and hilarious. It is rare. It holds both writers and readers in high esteem and is, as a result, the only show I know of that is watched by two different age groups of people with blue hair.

It's been suggested on occasion that *Imprint* goes above people's heads. Some, perhaps. Let me admit that, as host for three years there were times (when, for instance, those Foucaultian deconstructionists got out their lingual toolboxes) I was in over mine. But as a reader I have always responded to a challenge. I like to look up, I find it doesn't hurt to look up to great writers.

Oh. And how have the *writers* felt about the whole TV deal? Doubtless some of them have wanted to puke, micturate, etc. though no one actually said as such to me.

IRA NADEL,
excerpt

Leonard Cohen: A Life in Art

Leonard Cohen, the focus of Nadel's book (and the excerpt that follows), is the rarest of artists: someone whose work is received well by academic critics and by pop culture consumers. A poet and musician, Cohen has also quirkily overthrown another opposition: youth/age. In his early productive years he wrote fiction and poetry that were sometimes demanding intellectually and that spoke primarily to scholars and university students. In his fifties and sixties he became hip, cool—a sex symbol—with his raspy voice and romantic lyrics. Nadel, in *Leonard Cohen: A Life in Art*, gives the reader an overview of Cohen's life and his output. Published in 1994, it will need, of course, to be superseded or updated as Cohen continues to be a cultural force.

Questions:

1. Many facts/dates are provided. What research is involved in writing a biography of this kind?
2. What is the music/poetry connection that allows Cohen to go back and forth between the two?
3. Characterize Nadel's Cohen. Would someone else have produced a different Cohen?
4. What are the elements of Cohen's music that make it seductive?
5. Cohen is Jewish, yet he is attracted to Zen Buddhism. How have these dimensions of his life influenced his art?

Having moved to Los Angeles in order to spend at least six months each winter near his Zen master and the recording studios (the spring and summer, when not touring, Cohen usually spends in Montreal), he lives in a two-storey duplex, not far from the Jewish district surrounding Fairfax Avenue, that, at the time of *The Future*, he shared with his eighteen-year-old daughter, Lorca. His son, pursuing musical interests, divided his time between Montreal and his mother's apartment in Paris, although more recently he has attended Syracuse University.

Cohen has reported that he rarely ventures very far in Los Angeles, not much beyond a favoured Crenshaw-district café. During the 1992 riots, Cohen observed the destruction in south-central Los Angeles, seeing his grocery store, music-supply store, and electronics store all go up in flames. "From my balcony I could see five great fires. The air was thick with cinders." But he had expected this: "having been writing about such things for so long, it was not a surprise," he recently told an English reporter.

Cohen begins most days by visiting a *zendo*, a Zen Buddhist meditation centre, often rising at 4:30 a.m.; he then returns home to compose, deal with business matters, or swim. The house consists of a meditation room on the first floor and a former weight room; upstairs are his sparse quarters, painted and furnished in extreme white, the white of Hydra, with bleached floors. All is austerely furnished, including the bedroom, its only surprises being a black television, portable tape deck, and cd player. Surrounding a mirror in the hall is a collection of caps and hats. A menorah is evident on one of his several wooden tables, as well as the occasional gold candlestick. His workroom off the living room is, by contrast, high-tech, with a synthesizer, fax machine and Mac Classic computer that he often uses for freehand computer graphics. Here Cohen composes, arranges, and rearranges his music; "Closing Time" on *The Future* demonstrates this process well.

The song began as an up-tempo ballad but in its final form is something of a "demonic" square dance. Cohen has always been an enthusiastic and absorbed arranger, scoring and rescoring material through the difficult process of arranging, the musical equivalent to editing. The unexpected balance between the simplicity of the "Aegean bourgeois" and the complicated world of microchips creates an unusual artisanal atmosphere in the house. In Los Angeles, Cohen is close to musical associates, the recording studios, and, until recently, his companion Rebecca De Mornay, the actress he has been seeing since 1991. He dedicated *The Future* to her and acknowledged her assistance with the selections for *Stranger Music*. Robert Altman introduced them to each other some years ago. In crediting her with conceptualizing the sound on his recent record, Cohen cited a passage from Genesis 24 about virtuous Rebecca drawing water from a well for Abraham's thirsty servant.

The anguish that once characterized much of his work has been replaced by what Cohen more objectively calls "discomfort." But, as he adds, he is reluctant to discuss these matters "because they are essentially...of a religious nature, intimately connected to my work. That discomfort is refined in the crucible of attention and intuition and surrender, and what there is to say of it is in the work itself."

The November 1992 release of *The Future* dispelled all thought that Cohen's popularity had peaked. He planned originally to record the album in Montreal with the team that had produced *I'm Your Man*, but, when he went to Los Angeles to co-opt Warnes as a backup singer on "Democracy," he continued to work there and didn't leave for several years. He finds the city a dangerous but compelling locale. "It's a risky place to live....It's a place that's falling apart. Geologically, the ground is splitting." Yet, when telephoned in the spring of 1993 to see if he had survived a recent earthquake, he told the caller that he had been at the *zendo* when the tremors struck: "It was beautiful, man. Nobody broke position," he reported.

The Future was a hit with *Time, Rolling Stone, Stereo Review*, and other journals, as well as with the public, although the long tracks reduced its airtime on radio, a particular problem with Cohen's songs. "Democracy," in fact, is over seven minutes long; his campy version of "Always" is over eight. Nonetheless, the album sold more than 100,000 copies in Canada in its first four months, earning platinum status, and spawned an award-winning video for "Closing Time." Interviews appeared everywhere, and Cohen gladly shared with reporters and the public the background and four years of hard work on the album. And through it all, he maintained his cool, autographing a white leather shoe offered to him at the Toronto launch party for the album with his name and the sentence "Magic is afoot" from

Beautiful Losers. He frequently explained the genesis of his songs, including the centrepiece, "Democracy," an ironic paean to America; its fourth stanza reads:

> It's coming to America first,
> the cradle of the best and the worst.
> It's here they got the range
> and the machinery for change
> and it's here they got the spiritual thirst.
> It's here the family's broken
> and it's here the lonely say
> that the heart has got to open
> in a fundamental way:
> Democracy is coming to the U.S.A.

Marking the song's immediate popularity was its performance by Don Henley at the MTV ball in Washington during the January 1993 inauguration of President Bill Clinton.

Other remarkable songs on the album include a rummy version of Irving Berlin's "Always," recorded in the early hours of the morning in an isolated California studio, and a modern-day "Anthem," borrowing from Kabbalistic sources, especially the sixteenth-century Rabbi Isaac Luria, and expressing a critical idea of hope:

> Ring the bells that still can ring.
> Forget your perfect offering.
> There is a crack in everything.
> That's how the light gets in.

The rhythmic "Closing Time," and the pensive "Waiting for the Miracle" balance the essentially pessimistic opening song, "The Future." This political and moral declaration sets a powerful but negative tone for the album, which is quickly undercut by the desire to wait for the miracle, the next song. But the vision is dark, and the ironic wish to return to the totalitarian views of the past is represented by the closing verse, which defines *The Future* in one word: murder.

The blend of despair and hope in the album partly explains its appeal; so, too, does its musicianship. There is a professionalism and maturity in the sound that marks Cohen's eleventh album as a masterful expression of his vision, which is supported by lyrics of substance. Its positive reception initiated another European tour throughout the late spring and summer of 1993: Europe, then New York, Washington, Toronto, Winnipeg, Vancouver, and Victoria, ending in Los Angeles at the Wiltern Theatre on 5 July, although extended bookings in Canada took Cohen back there in late July 1993.

Recognitions continued to accrue: McGill University awarded Cohen an honorary degree on 16 June 1992 (appropriately, Bloomsday, the date of Joyce's *Ulysses*), with Louis Dudek, his former professor and "literary godfather," presenting him to the chancellor for conferral. A November 1992 *New York Times* article praises Cohen as "a singular entity: a kind of rock-and-roll Lord Byron, a cultural scholar in the unlikely medium of pop." On 21 March 1993, Cohen received the Male Vocalist of the Year Award at the Juno Awards ceremony in Toronto. He also won the award for best video for "Closing Time," set in a Toronto honky-tonk bar, the Matador Club, owned by Cohen's friend Ann Dunn. A recent article on him in *The New Yorker* underscores the Cohen phenomenon, emphasizing his resiliency and persistent appeal to generations of listeners, which a writer in *Maclean's* nicely summarizes: "Although he has occasionally faded from the scene, he has never really fallen from fashion."

A one hour CBC Radio show entitled "The Gospel According to Leonard Cohen," broadcast 12 September 1993, highlighted an interview conducted in Montreal, supported by cuts from his best-known songs. The interview surveyed his spiritual views and confirmed his identity as a "minstrel." This broadcast anticipated more public attention with the announcement on 5 October 1993 that Cohen had won a Governor General's Performing Arts Award for his contribution to Canadian music. Formal presentation of the ten-thousand-dollar award was made in Ottawa on 26 November by Governor General Ramon Hnatyshyn, followed by a gala the next evening, at the National Arts Centre, that celebrated the achievements of Cohen and the seven other winners.

The publication in Canada on 13 November 1993 of *Stranger Music: Selected Poems and Songs* marked a plateau in Cohen's writing career. The 415-page book is comprised of selections from his formerly out-of-print poetry supplemented by the lyrics to many of his songs. Appearing also in the United States and Great Britain, it is the first of his books dedicated to his children, Adam and Lorca. The poems and songs were chosen by several friends, but Cohen approved the selections and, in some cases, reworked them. Yet they stand as an important, one-volume reminder of the union of poet and songwriter, which have never been separated for him. The recent publication of *Beautiful Losers* in an American paperback has also enlarged his readership. Cohen has commented that "it's very agreeable at 58 to see these books you wrote at 25, 28. I'm delighted. You do have that sense of vindication somehow. You do feel that you're standing in that long tradition of people who were really misunderstood in their time and then re-discovered."

Virtually coinciding with the publication of *Stranger Music* was the first conference in Canada held exclusively on Cohen and his work, a two-and-a-half-day gathering in Red Deer, Alberta (22–24 October 1993), which drew critics, writers, and musicians, including one of his current backup singers, Perla Batalla. During the time spent debating, criticizing, and admiring Cohen's work, videos and films by and about Cohen played continuously. Papers from the conference appeared in a special issue of *Canadian Poetry* (1993) devoted to him. These and other events underscore the academic as well as public recognition of Cohen, which his fans acknowledged long ago.

In constantly underscoring the need for a spiritual existence in an irreligious time, Cohen marks out a special place of dignity, paralleled by his engagement with the virtually holy act of writing and composing. Hence his posture in the cover photo of *Stranger*

Music: his head bent down in contemplation, he sits cross-legged in a Buddhist pose, suggestively suspended over the ground and clearly uninterested in the viewer's gaze. He is spiritually self-absorbed. Only discipline and self-exploration, he has repeated, can supplant his often bone-dry creativity in contrast to other, more productive artists. While it may take Dylan only fifteen minutes to write a song, it takes Cohen years: "You shatter versions of the self until you get down to a line, a word, that you can defend, that you can wrap your voice around without choking," he declared.

"My Life in Art" is a deliberately chosen title for the statements in *Death of a Lady's Man*. Yet with this awareness of the commitment to poetry and song comes the humbleness (successor to the victimization) that also defines Cohen's work and performances. Before the power of the voice and the word—and what they can convey—Cohen stands with bowed head and gratitude because he understands the responsibility of creation and the integrity required to make a work honest. Judaism, Yoga, Buddhism, fasting, vegetarianism, love, drugs, poetry, song, painting—all are steps in his search for the freedom of simplicity. But Cohen also knows that not everyone can experience this freedom; consequently, he constantly offers thanks to those who attempt to comprehend him as he attempts to break down the barriers between listener and performer, stage and audience—as he tries to stand aside from the words and to let their power speak, thereby allowing the newsreel to become the feature, as he writes in *Beautiful Losers*. In the first phase of his career, life and its ritual symbols formed his art, providing the substance for, and shape of, his writing; in the second, art, as symbolic and religious expression, has fashioned his life.

Once asked if he liked himself, Cohen replied—after a pause—that he liked only his "true self," which he has constantly sought to discover. Through his art, spiritual journeys, romantic relationships, and retreats, he continues to define himself. But the feelings that he studies, he masters, thus providing an integrity for all that he undertakes. He remains a figure of spirit, decorum, and intensity, managing to make sadness into a career, say the ungenerous, and to elevate despair to understanding, say his admirers. Art, united with the recognition of the necessity of spirit in a world inhospitable to its presence, has been the means for Leonard Cohen to join the coordinates of his life.

SAMIR GANDESHA,

"New York City Man"

Just two years ago, I (Stan Fogel, one of this reader's editors) was the external examiner of a University of Toronto Ph.D. dissertation in English literature that studied the work of Lou Reed(!). Alongside Shakespeare and Hemingway as objects of study, then, Lou Reed has taken his place in the halls of academe. Indeed, as the article below makes clear, Reed's famous song "Heroin" was written under the influence of...(you thought I was going to write "drugs")...the American poet and teacher Delmore Schwartz. This article is representative of much academic writing and journalism that goes under the name of cultural studies. It treats rockers as seriously as it does poets!

Questions:

1. Note how Gandesha cites a good many influential literary and political figures in order to boost Reed's image.
2. Do you listen to Reed's music? If so, how well does Gandesha describe his music and his influence?
3. Compare Gandesha's portrait of N.Y. with Bayoumi's earlier in the reader.
4. According to Gandesha, what role do drugs play in Reed's music?
5. There is now a great deal of academic material on pop music. Does it enhance your appreciation of the music...or just clutter it with verbiage?

In a celebrated essay on Charles Baudelaire, Walter Benjamin defines the creative process as resulting from the attempt to mitigate the heady "shock effects" of the modern metropolis; Lou Reed's relationship with New York City, both real and imagined, can be characterized in the same way. Reed's confrontation with New York embodies a minimalism that finds its architectural analogue in the international style of that city's built environment. In its almost cinematic visuality, the music expresses at the same time that it absorbs the impact of urban experience. While Baudelaire's writings capture the rhythms and textures of the newly constructed boulevards of Haussmann's Paris, for Reed the shock effects of New York were painfully and literally immediate. When he was 17, he was subjected to electro-shock therapy at Creedmore State Mental hospital—documented in "Kill Your Sons"—aimed at normalizing a kid who had developed what his parents considered to be an excessively feminine demeanor. Electroshock therapy was a formative experience for Reed; it was a reflection of the suburban dystopia of Long Island. He would shrewdly turn the treatment in an anti-institutional direction to elude the draft in 1964. While Baudelaire brought the deft precision of a lyric poet to the boulevard, Reed raises the street, the world of the junkie, the sociopath, the hipster and the drag queen to poetry. The work of both artists is oriented towards capturing the eternal moment in the transitory flux and flow of urban experience. As Reed explains: "In New York City I can pick up a phone and have anything I want delivered to the door. I can step outside the door and get into a fight immediately. All the energy, people going crazy, guys with no legs on roller skates. It's very intense, the energy level is incredible."

In 1989, Reed released what many critics held to be his most important album since *Berlin*, produced over a decade and a half earlier; appropriately, it was entitled *New York*. What was so striking about this work was that while *Berlin* was a concept album centered on the violent psycho-sexual politics of a disintegrating relationship, *New York*, also thematically unified, addresses the political landscape of New York City and through it what Reed described as "that savage jungle called America" in an era of an ascendant neo-conservatism. If *Berlin* evoked a city divided at the time by the Iron Curtain, then *New York* was the document of a city that had come to be increasingly driven by racial, ethnic and class divisions. One of the most compelling tracks of the album, "Hold On," was reprinted in the op-ed pages of the *New York Times* under the title "Anarchy in the Streets." The album traces the transformations the city undergoes through the late 1970s and 1980s. After facing bankruptcy in the 1970s as a result of the repeated blows sustained to its industrial sector after the Oil Crisis, towards the late-1980s New York experienced a tremendous economic boom. It was not, however, a boom from which all New Yorkers benefitted. The city became increasingly characterized by massive inequalities between the rich—financial and real estate speculators such as Ivan Boesky and Donald Trump and slumlords like Leona Helmsley—and the poor, many of whom were and still are being driven out onto the streets. New York came to be pervaded by increasing levels of homelessness, divisions between contending racial and ethnic groups and an intractable AIDS crisis which was wreaking havoc on the Christopher Street gay community and on intravenous drug users alike. *New York* was a step in an entirely different direction for Reed; the "Rock'n'Roll Animal" had become a political animal.

New York's social criticism is expressed as much through its raw lyrics as in its ability to stretch three chords to the point where they would release as yet unheard possibilities; a minimalism stripped so bare that it enabled all of the diverse cadences of the city to be heard. This formal tension between constraint and the freedom which it, paradoxically, makes possible is one which infuses all of Reed's work. "Dirty Boulevard," for instance, deconstructs the image of New York City as the gateway to the American Dream which finds its inscription on the city's most recognizable landmark, the Statue of Liberty: "Give me your hungry, your tired, your poor I'll piss on them/That's what the statue of Bigotry says/Your poor huddled masses—let's club 'em to death/and get it over with and just dump 'em on the

Boulevard." In the blink of an eye, the myth of America as the "Land of the Free," as a classless society, resolves into two separate realities, one for the rich and one for the poor. "Outside it's a bright night, there's an opera at Lincoln Center/movie stars arrive by limousine/The klieg lights shoot up over the skyline of Manhattan/but the lights are out on the mean streets." Despite the fact that he lives in squalor with nine siblings, and endures regular beatings from his father, Pedro, the protagonist of the song, has not completely relinquished hope for a better life: "he's found a book on magic in a garbage can/He looks at the pictures and stares up at the crooked ceiling/At the count of three, he says, I hope I can disappear and fly fly away...."

New York's unearthing of the shattered fragments of the American Dream in the 1980s makes clear how so much of Reed's vision of New York City, with its unflinching eye for the often sociopathic realities lurking in the shadows of the opulent Manhattan city scape—pointing back to earlier work such as "Street Hassle" and "Kicks"—actually embodies at a much deeper level the possibility of freedom. From early on in his career, well before he would write himself into the mythology of the city, Reed portrays New York City—as only a queer Jewish kid from Freeport, Long Island could—as a place of redemption. "Rock'n'Roll," from the Velvet Underground's last studio album, *Loaded*, contrasts the "computations" and "amputations" of the suburbs with the city: "Then one fine mornin' she put on a New York station/And she couldn't believe what she heard at all/ She started dancin' to that fine fine music/You know her life was saved by Rock'n'Roll." The original version of this song, released for the first time in 1986 on Velvet Underground's *Another View*, features a startlingly seraphic reprise following the last steely chord change: "And it was all right. It was all right."

In "Heroin," a song that Reed had written under the spell of the poet Delmore Schwartz at Syracuse University, the freedom the city offers is inextricable from a crushing, physical necessity. As Reed put it, "I take drugs because in the twentieth century in a technological age, living in the city, there are certain drugs you can take just to keep you normal."Or, as he once related to Angie Bowie, "The atmosphere is so polluted that you have to put chemicals in your body to counteract it." As the tempo of "Heroin" kicks in and quickens, once the smack begins to flow, its warming rush through the blood stream, while initially establishing equilibrium, quickly changes direction and becomes overwhelming. Thus, while it becomes a principal means of parrying the accelerated pace of urban experience, the narcotic nonetheless becomes intrinsic to the very experience that needs to be parried.

It is ironic that Lou Reed has come to be closely associated with heroin, while his drug of choice since his days at Syracuse had been speed or methamphetamine hydrochloride, whose effects differ quite radically from the deadening euphoria of the opiate. Speed alters the functioning of the synapses in the brain, quickening speech, heightening perception and bolstering desire. Speed becomes a kind of technology, permitting the body to function at higher levels of productivity, enabling it to go for days at a time without sleep. As Punk was to make clear a few years later, speed was the quintessential urban drug in that it mimics and enhances the furious pace of the metropolis. As Reed suggests: "It's nice at five in the morning to be stoned on THC and go down to Hong Fows, have some watercress soup, then you take a taxi uptown with some maniac and say, 'Go ahead drive fast, wise guy,' and you just zip around. When you go up to Park Avenue, there's a very funny turn and its always funny to wonder if they'll make it."

A specifically New York vision of urban experience permits us retrospectively to re-evaluate the latent politics of Reed's earliest work. Today, in an era in which "transgression" has become the mantra of progressive intellectuals, the media routinely offer advice on S/M and B/D sex practices and trans-sexuals are the flavour of the month in the academy, it is difficult to grasp how subversive Reed's work actually was. It is no small irony that at the very moment street culture has become co-opted by the mainstream, the mean streets of New York are being sanitized by Rudolph Giuliani. That Reed himself has become very much part of the rock'n'roll establishment is beyond question. For instance, in the mid-1980s Reed, symbolically and otherwise, put considerable distance between himself and the street by doing an ad for Honda motor scooters in which he declared "Don't settle for walking." Nonetheless, there can be no doubt that his speed-freak persona from the early 1970s—peroxide-blond cropped hair, emaciated, clad in black leather, shooting up on stage—has to be one of the most powerful and enduring images of rock'n'roll's negativity, its ability to confront bourgeois society with its own nihilistic image. While the corporate world has had no trouble appropriating the counter-culture of the 1960s—much detested by Reed and John Cale—it seems improbable that the early-1970s incarnation of Lou Reed could ever be used to sell banking services. Perhaps it was this very aloofness from explicit political engagement that, in an age in which the very notion of transgression has become normalized, gives Reed's work such tremendous political force.

The delayed anti-institutional effect of Reed's work became especially clear during the movement that led to the ultimate demise of the authoritarian regime in then Czechoslovakia in 1989, a revolution that brought the dissident playwright, Vaclav Havel, to power. As Havel makes clear in an interview conducted by Reed, himself, he was in New York for anti-war protests in the Summer of 1968—around the time that the Soviets were in the process of crushing the "Prague Spring." While in New York, Havel acquired the Velvet Underground's second album. *White Light/White Heat*—whose most important track, "Sister Ray," was to have, via the Modern Lovers' "Road Runner," a direct influence on the Sex Pistols—and took it back to Prague with him. From that point onward, the music of Velvet Underground was to become integral to the non-conformist spirit of dissent in the political underground of that country and inspired one of the first Czech rock bands, The Plastic People of the Universe, at a time when rock'n'roll music was strictly proscribed by the regime. This was a "Velvet Revolution" indeed.

Style

INSTEAD OF THE TRADITIONAL notion that it is something we add to our "true" selves, style, in our "pomo" world, has come to be seen as comprising our identities. It's not only that "we are what we eat"; we're also what we wear, say, even believe…and these are drawn from such elements as fashion creators, advertisers, religious leaders, professors and the media. In short, our style is us, whether it's, say, flamboyant punk or Lauren conservative. In these pieces that follow, food, home and hair are all subject to the kind of scrutiny that reveals the social and cultural conditioning involved in what we eat, where we live and what hairstyles we choose. I don't know if the slang phrase "free, white and twenty-one" means anything anymore—anyway, it shouldn't. "Free" is obviously a relative term that some interpret in an era of globalization as "free to buy the brand of your choice"; white, as we said in an earlier section, is hardly a universal term; finally, the age of majority varies, depending on where you live.

JOANNE KATES,

"For the Love of the Cheese"

Joanne Kates is a food writer who does to restaurant reviewing what "nouvelle cuisine" chefs do to the meals you get in fine restaurants—she and they produce art! To those on student (or working persons') budgets who don't get to nibble sea bass tartare, hamachi baked in a banana leaf or lentil millefeuille, all presented with a nod towards Matisse, not the microwave, Kates's prose will have to do. The author's homage to Leo Bertozzi, who (as she writes) did his Ph.D. dissertation on parmesan cheese, reveals a love of research, a love of food...and a love of prose in the service of gourmet products.

Questions:

1. There is a proliferation of alliteration herein. Does this make your mouth water?
2. Note the doctor metaphor that further ennobles the cheesemaker's art.
3. Here, too, short sentences seem to work effectively. To what end?
4. The exactness of Kates's reportage matches the exactness of the cheese-making process. Discuss the parallels.
5. Do you think the cheese burger deserves the kind of testimonial Kates gives parmesan cheese?

Leo Bertozzi did his doctoral thesis on what you and I would call parmesan cheese. He spent two years studying the effect of cow versus calf rennet on the cheese, when used to help the curds and whey separate. Calf is better. And the right name of the cheese is *parmigiano reggiano*, which is made around Parma in an area no bigger than seventy square miles. Let someone from outside the area, or a dairy taking shortcuts, advertise cheese by that name: the possible penalty is a year in jail, and the parmigiano consortium, where Leo Bertozzi got a job after graduation, is a careful parmigiano policeman. Parmigiano reggiano, the real thing, is so precious that in inflationary times Parmenese store it in bank vaults. Unlike paper money, its value never falls.

Italians take their parmigiano seriously. It is 9 a.m. at one of the 1017 parmigiano dairies, and a woman is soaking her broken leg in a bucket of hot whey. In ten big copper cauldrons, milk steams. Leo Bertozzi says: "In America you are afraid of sickness, so copper is forbidden for cheesemaking." Parmenese have been cooking their cheese in copper cauldrons for seven centuries and thus far they seem to have survived it. It is only since the war that electricity has replaced wood fires under the cauldrons. But certain things never change.

Every night the evening's unpasteurized milk is brought to the dairy and left overnight to rest. In the morning the morning milk is mixed with it, but not just slam bam thank you ma'am. Each farm sends its milk in cans, not a tanker truck, so the cheesemaker, who knows the unique taste of each farmer's milk, can mix and match to get the cheese flavour he wants.

The milk is piped into the cauldrons, twelve hundred kilos of milk per cauldron. The cheesemaker's wife weighs out rennet, from the lining of milk-fed calves' stomachs, and they add it, along with some of yesterday's whey, to encourage fermentation. The milk separates into curds and whey. The cheesemakers stir to break up the curds. They cook it and the grainy curd (*grana*) settles into a mass at the bottom of the cauldron. Now the cheese has to come out of the pot, but you don't want to shock it. So you wait just the right amount of time till the milk is cool enough, and then scoop up the cheese from the bottom with a long wooden paddle. It lumbers to the surface like a huge white sponge. Another man gets a cheesecloth sling under the cheese, and cuts it in half with a long knife. And now there are two embryonic parmigiano cheeses. It takes six hundred kilos of milk (the milk from almost fifty cows) to make one cheese, and most of the dairies produce fewer than ten cheeses every day, because that's all one cheesemaker can do. Most cheesemakers will not permit another cheesemaker in their dairies, so expansion is impossible. This dairy is an exception, a veritable multicorp: they make twenty cheeses every day, because there are two cheesemakers, a man and his brother-in-law. With two wives to wash the cheesecloth and weigh the rennet.

The two men lift the cheeses out of the cauldron in their cheesecloth slings, and hang them on wooden rods to drip dry all day. There are twenty-six hundred pigs in the barn out back; they're waiting for the whey that will be pumped to them. There's a piggery attached to every parmigiano dairy, for eating whey makes pig flesh sweet like honey, and all those pigs will one day be prosciutto, a.k.a. Parma ham.

At eleven o'clock that night each cheese is put into a round wooden mold with a plastic liner that has raised letters on it. The letters spell out the words parmigiano reggiano, the cheese's date of birth, and which copper cauldron it was born in. The cheeses spend the second day of their lives in metal molds, and on the third day they're gently lowered into big vats of brine. The brine room looks like Junior Red Cross for cheeses, each one bobbing in line by its neighbour. They are turned every day. Any cheeses with delinquent tendencies to float unevenly are hauled out of the pool. Because the cauldron number is stamped on the cheese the cheesemaker can figure out which farm its milk came from. If it floats funny he trouble-shoots with the farmer.

After three or four weeks (depending on the weather) in the bath the pubescent parmigianos move to the adolescent aging room, where they sit on wooden shelves with little drops of sweat beading on their fresh young flesh. The air has a nutty sweet scent. Please God, lock me in.

A month later the cheeses move to the main aging room, which is to be their home for two years. From floor to ceiling, a thirty-five-foot height, are parmigiano cheeses, fifteen thousand of them, not dead but sleeping. This cheese is a living thing. The germs grow; fermentation occurs. The skin darkens. The flavour deepens.

Every week a robot turns and dusts each cheese, but only a human can truly babysit it. The cheeses need air to breathe, but if the air moves too quickly over them their skin will dry too fast. If it's too warm they perspire, and if it's too cold they can't ripen. Air conditioning works fine for industrial cheeses, but it's too cold for parmigiano. The cheesemaker is the babysitter. In summer he shuts the windows to keep the heat out. Every night he opens them again to give the cheeses fresh air. But if a storm comes up the cheesemaker gets out of bed, no matter the time, and closes the windows. As birth attendant to one of the greatest cheeses in the world, this is his duty.

After its first year every single parmigiano cheese is tested by the consortium. A cheese doctor hammers it all over to listen to its heart: a hollow sound is a fault, a sign of air. More tests are done on cheeses with faults. The cheese doctor inserts a needle into the cheese to do a biopsy. He smells it, tastes it, decides whether this cheese deserves the parmigiano reggiano title, or must be relegated to the farm team and sold as "grana" or "parmesan," nameless grating cheese. They know that if a cheese has survived a summer, it'll make it. Those that pass the test are branded like cows and sent back to rest and mature till they're two.

Bright young fellows with Yankee know-how have come to Parma and tried to streamline things. In the 1970s they collected the milk in tanker trucks for a time. But the cheesemakers rebelled. The milk was jostled too much in transit. The opportunity to custom-mix the milk from different farms was lost. The cheese suffered. So they switched back to the small cans. If he wanted to make cheese efficiently, says Leo Bertozzi, he would "pasteurize the milk and keep it at the farm for four or five days. I'd bring it to the dairy in big tanks. I would use a cow with a high yield, and feed the cows silage instead of the grass and hay we use. I'd make a cheese in a month instead of two years." Silage is fermented feed kept in silos. The cows get bacteria from it, so their milk must be pasteurized or treated with antiseptic or nitrates. Feeding silage to these cows would be like using margarine to make shortbread. If you doubt Dr. Bertozzi's word, go to your neighbourhood cheese store. Buy one hunk of what is called parmesan cheese and another of parmigiano reggiano, which many local stores sell. If you can't see the two words on the big round's rind, don't buy it. Do a blind tasting. Write me a letter. I'm with Bertozzi.

The cheesemakers are conservative. Whenever a change is proposed by Bertozzi and his nine colleagues in the consortium lab, they ask: "What will it do to the cheese?" Only twenty years ago milking machines were adopted. The cheesemakers were afraid something would be lost, and they were right. When you milk by hand you get bacteria from your hands, some of which are beneficial. The big dairy farms with spotless milking parlours have to add bacteria because their milk has, in Bertozzi's sad words, "no life."

To be a cheesemaker means to be in love with the cheese, to have the cheese and the milk in your blood. Bertozzi says: "If you want to make cheddar cheese or cottage cheese you go to school to learn, but this cheese you can't learn in school." Cheesemakers are born here. Children grow up in the dairy and they learn to mix the milk by taste, to cook the curd with one hand in it and the other controlling the temperature, when to take the cheese from the brine bath and when to leave it longer. Most cheesemakers quit school and go into the dairy full-time around the age of ten. This sense cannot be taught in manuals, nor can the peculiar dedication of the parmigiano families. The life of a cheesemaker is completely taken by his work, by the pigs, by the milk, by the love of cheese. Nothing else exists. They do not trust anyone else to care for their cheeses, and the cheeses require daily attention. There are no vacations, you're never sick, there are no days off. There are Parmenese cheesemakers who haven't missed a day since they returned from the front in 1945. Their cheese is their honour. Leo Bertozzi worries: "How long will we find these people? When the cheesemakers' sons see that other people take vacations and have free evenings, what will they do? It's completely opposite to the way of the world."

WITOLD RYBCZYNSKI,
excerpt

Home: A Short History of an Idea

This article, which integrates architecture, philosophy and sociology, could have ended up as the kind of thing only academic specialists read. Instead, Rybczynski, here and elsewhere, writes essays that are both accessible and intellectually challenging. Concepts such as comfort are difficult to write about because they are so vast, yet Rybczynski has the knack of being able to give them specificity and to discuss them in a lively fashion. Comfort, in these few pages, gets defined and historicized; it also gets narrowed to enhance Rybczynski's more extended focus: home. Not only is comfort what he writes about; it also is more often than not the state readers are in when sampling Rybczynski's prose.

Questions:

1. How does the author achieve the comfort level indicated above?
2. What tactics would you use to engage a term such as comfort—or confidence, individuality, strength…?
3. Compare scientific to other methods of assessment and evaluation.
4. Examine the onion simile Rybczynski uses.
5. What is comfort to you?

What is comfort? The simplest response would be that comfort concerns only human physiology—feeling good. Nothing mysterious about that. But this would not explain why, although the human body has not changed, our idea of what is comfortable differs from that of a hundred years ago. Nor is the answer that comfort is a subjective experience of satisfaction. If comfort were subjective, one would expect a greater variety of attitudes toward it; instead, at any particular historical period there has always been a demonstrable consensus about what is comfortable and what is not. Although comfort is experienced personally, the individual judges comfort according to broader norms, indicating that comfort may be an objective experience.

If comfort is objective, it should be possible to measure it. This is more difficult than it sounds. It is easier to know when we are comfortable than why, or to what degree. It would be possible to identify comfort by recording the personal reactions of large numbers of people, but this would be more like a marketing or opinion survey than a scientific study; a scientist prefers to study things one at a time, and especially to measure them. It turns out that in practice it is much easier to measure discomfort than comfort. To establish a thermal "comfort zone," for example, one ascertains at which temperatures most people are either too cold or too hot, and whatever is in between automatically becomes "comfortable." Or if one is trying to identify the appropriate angle for the back of a chair, one can subject people to angles that are too steep and too flat, and between the points where they express discomfort lies the "correct" angle. Similar experiments have been carried out concerning the intensity of lighting and noise, the size of room dimensions, the hardness and softness of sitting and lying furniture, and so on. In all these cases, the range of comfort is discovered by measuring the limits at which people begin to experience discomfort. When the interior of the Space Shuttle was being designed, a cardboard mock-up of the cabin was built. The astronauts were required to move around in this full-size model, miming their daily activities, and every time they knocked against a corner or a projection, a technician would cut away the offending piece. At the end of the process, when there were no more obstructions left, the cabin was judged to be "comfortable." The scientific definition of comfort would be something like "Comfort is that condition in which discomfort has been avoided."

Most of the scientific research that has been carried out on terrestrial comfort has concerned the workplace, since it has been found that comfortable surroundings will affect the morale, and hence the productivity, of workers. Just how much comfort can affect economic performance is indicated by a recent estimate that backaches—the result of poor working posture—account for over ninety-three million lost workdays, a loss of nine billion dollars to the American economy. The modern office interior reflects the scientific definition of comfort. Lighting levels have been carefully controlled to fall within an acceptable level for optimal reading convenience. The finishes of walls and floors are restful; there are no garish or gaudy colors. Desks and chairs are planned to avoid fatigue.

But how comfortable do the people feel who work in such surroundings? As part of an effort to improve its facilities, one large pharmaceutical corporation, Merck & Company, surveyed two thousand of its office staff regarding their attitudes to their place of work—an attractive modern commercial interior. The survey team prepared a questionnaire that listed various aspects of the workplace. These included factors affecting appearance, safety, work efficiency, convenience, comfort, and so on. Employees were asked to express their satisfaction, or dissatisfaction, with different aspects, and also to indicate those aspects that they personally considered to be the most important. The majority distinguished between the visual qualities of their surroundings—decoration, color scheme, carpeting, wall covering, desk appearance—and the physical aspects—lighting, ventilation, privacy, and chair comfort. The latter group were all included in a list of the ten most important factors, together with size of work area, safety, and personal storage space. Interestingly, none of the purely visual factors was felt to be of major importance, indicating just how mistaken is the notion that comfort is solely a function of appearance or style.

What is most revealing is that the Merck employees expressed some degree of dissatisfaction with *two-thirds* of the almost thirty different aspects of the workplace. Among those about which there was the strongest negative feelings were the lack of conversational privacy, the air quality, the lack of visual privacy, and the level of lighting. When they were asked what aspects of the office interior they would like to have individual control over, most people identified room temperature, degree of privacy, choice of chair and desk, and lighting intensity. Control over decor was accorded the lowest priority. This would seem to indicate that although there is wide agreement about the importance of lighting or temperature, there is a good deal of difference of opinion about exactly how much light or heat feels comfortable to different individuals; comfort is obviously both objective and subjective.

The Merck offices had been designed to eliminate discomfort, yet the survey showed that many of the employees did not experience well-being in their workplace—an inability to concentrate was the common complaint. Despite the restful colors and the attractive furnishings (which everyone appreciated), something was missing. The scientific approach assumes that if background noises are muffled and direct view controlled, the office worker will feel comfortable. But working comfort depends on many more factors than these. There must also be a sense of intimacy and privacy, which is produced by a balance between isolation and publicness; too much of one or the other will produce discomfort. A group of architects in California recently identified as many as nine different aspects of workplace enclosure that must be met in order to create this feeling. These included the presence of walls behind and beside the worker, the amount of open space in front of the desk, the area of the workspace, the amount of enclosure, a view to the outside, the distance to the nearest person, the number of people in the immediate vicinity, and the level and type of noise. Since most office layouts do not address these concerns directly, it is not surprising that people have difficulty concentrating on their work.

The fallacy of the scientific definition of comfort is that it considers only those aspects of comfort that are measurable, and with not untypical arrogance denies the existence of the rest—many behavioral scientists have concluded that because people experience only discomfort, comfort as a physical phenomenon does not really exist at all. It is hardly surprising that genuine intimacy, which is impossible to measure, is absent in most planned office environments. Intimacy in the office, or in the home, is not unusual in this respect; there are many complicated experiences that resist measurement. It is impossible, for example, to describe scientifically what distinguishes a great wine from a mediocre one, although a group of wine experts would have no difficulty establishing which was which. The wine industry, like manufacturers of tea and coffee, continues to rely on nontechnical testing—the "nose" of an experienced taster—rather than on objective standards alone. It might be possible to measure a threshold below which wine would taste "bad"—acidity, alcohol content, sweetness, and so on—but no one would suggest that simply avoiding these deficiencies would result in a good wine. A room may feel uncomfortable—it may be too bright for intimate conversation, or too dark for reading—but avoiding such irritations will not automatically produce a feeling of well-being. Dullness is not annoying enough to be disturbing, but it is not stimulating either. On the other hand, when we open a door and think, "What a comfortable room," we are reacting positively to something special, or rather to a series of special things.

Here are two descriptions of comfort. The first is by a well-known interior decorator, Billy Baldwin: "Comfort to me is a room that works for you and your guests. It's deep upholstered furniture. It's having a table handy to put down a drink or a book. It's also knowing that if someone pulls up a chair for a talk, the whole room doesn't fall apart. I'm tired of contrived decorating." The second is by an architect, Christopher Alexander: "Imagine yourself on a winter afternoon with a pot of tea, a book, a reading light, and two or three huge pillows to lean back against. Now make yourself comfortable. Not in some way which you can show to other people, and say how much you like it. I mean so that you *really* like it, for *yourself.* You put the tea where you can reach it: but in a place where you can't possibly knock it over. You pull the light down, to shine on the book, but not too brightly, and so that you can't see the naked bulb. You put the cushions behind you, and place them, carefully, one by one, just where you want them, to support your back, your neck, your arm: so that you are supported comfortably, just as you want to sip your tea, and read, and dream." Baldwin's description was the result of sixty years of decorating fashionable homes; Alexander's was based on the observation of ordinary people and ordinary places. Yet Baldwin, until his death in 1983, was generally considered to be the foremost high-society decorator; his clients included Cole Porter and Jacqueline Kennedy. Alexander is the author of the iconoclastic A *Pattern Language,* a critique of modern architecture. They both seem to have converged in the depiction of a domestic atmosphere that is instantly recognizable for its ordinary, human qualities.

These qualities are something that science has failed to come to grips with, although to the layman a picture, or a written description, is evidence enough. "Comfort is simply a verbal invention," writes one engineer despairingly. Of course, that is precisely what comfort is. It is an invention—a cultural artifice. Like all cultural ideas—childhood, family, gender—it has a past, and it cannot be understood without reference to its specific history. One-dimensional, technical definitions of comfort, which ignore history, are bound to be unsatisfactory. How rich, by comparison, are Baldwin's and Alexander's descriptions of comfort. They include convenience (a handy table), efficiency (a modulated light source), domesticity (a cup of tea), physical ease (deep chairs and cushions), and privacy (reading a book, having a talk). Intimacy is also present in these descriptions. All these characteristics together contribute to the atmosphere of interior calm that is a part of comfort.

This is the problem with understanding comfort and with finding a simple definition. It is like trying to describe an onion. It appears simple on the outside, just a spheroidal shape. But this is deceptive, for an onion also has many layers. If we cut it apart, we are left with a pile of onion skins, but the original form has disappeared; if we describe each layer separately, we lose sight of the whole. To complicate matters further, the layers are transparent, so that when we look at the whole onion we see not just the surface but also something of the interior. Similarly, comfort is both something simple and complicated. It incorporates many transparent layers of meaning—privacy, ease, convenience—some of which are buried deeper than others.

The onion simile suggests not only that comfort has several layers of meaning, but also that the idea of comfort has developed historically. It is an idea that has meant different things at different times. In the seventeenth century, comfort meant privacy, which led to intimacy and, in turn, to domesticity. The eighteenth century shifted the emphasis to leisure and ease, the nineteenth to mechanically aided comforts—light, heat, and ventilation. The twentieth-century domestic engineers stressed efficiency and convenience. At various times, and in response to various outside forces—social, economic, and technological—the idea of comfort has changed, sometimes drastically. There was nothing foreordained or inevitable about the changes. If seventeenth-century Holland had been less egalitarian and its women less independent, domesticity would have arrived later than it did. If eighteenth-century England had been aristocratic rather than bourgeois, comfort would have taken a different turn. But what is striking is that the idea of comfort, even as it has changed, has preserved most of its earlier meanings. The evolution of comfort should not be confused with the evolution of technology. New technical devices usually—not always—rendered older ones obsolete. The electric lamp replaced the gasolier, which replaced the oil lamp, which replaced candles, and so on. But new ideas about how to achieve comfort did not displace fundamental notions of domestic well-being. Each new meaning added a layer to the previous meanings, which were preserved beneath. At any particular time, comfort consists of *all* the layers, not only the most recent.

So there it is, the Onion Theory of Comfort—hardly a definition at all, but a more precise explanation may be unnecessary. It may be enough to realize that domestic comfort involves a range of attributes—convenience, efficiency, leisure, ease, pleasure, domesticity, intimacy, and privacy—all of which contribute to the experience; common sense will do the rest. Most people—"I may not know why I like it, but I know what I like"—recognize comfort when they experience it. This recognition involves a combination of sensations—many of them subconscious—and not only physical, but also emotional as well as intellectual, which makes comfort difficult to explain and impossible to measure. But it does not make it any less real. We should resist the inadequate definitions that engineers and architects have offered us. Domestic well-being is too important to be left to experts; it is, as it has always been, the business of the family and the individual. We must rediscover for ourselves the mystery of comfort, for without it, our dwellings will indeed be machines instead of homes.

LAURA MILLARD,

"Images of Canada: Canadian Bank Notes"

It's probably difficult to imagine a duller topic than the art on Canadian banknotes and what that art indicates about our country. Laura Millard, however, provides an interesting, smoothly written account of our national identity and character as they are "read" from our money. Her article offers a good example of "cultural studies"—which might be defined as the examination of culture and society as if they were literary texts. Political dimensions of that social text are, as often as not, revealed in the undertaking. The combination of technology and art that, for Millard, generates our bills gets close scrutiny here. Her method allows students the opportunity to "read" tenaciously seemingly insignificant aspects of our world.

Questions:

1. What do our banknotes reveal about our self-imaging? How about our recent "new" 10s—can you read them?
2. The premise here is that governments, like all other institutions and agencies, are involved in self-promotion. Discuss.
3. The author was teaching at the Nova Scotia School of Art and Design when she wrote this article. Discuss the current importance of design in our culture. Can you relate this to the design of your own writing?

4. "Banknotes are worth getting to know better." Are you motivated to examine them more carefully?
5. This article is less flamboyantly written than many of the others in this collection. How would you characterize Millard's style?

"The nature of our government, our bilingual heritage and the diversity of Canada's geography and wildlife are emphasized by the portraits, legends, landscapes, birds and national symbols which appear on every bank note."

This quotation from the display text in the "Paper Puzzles" exhibition at the Currency Museum in Ottawa states that aspects of our "nature" as Canadians are emphasized through the appearance of our bank notes and suggests that every note provides a cryptic combination of elements which signify "Canada." The text goes on to say, "Bank notes are worth getting to know better—not only because of their value but because of the fascinating secrets they have to tell." The key for unlocking these secrets, however, is not provided by official texts.

Just as our nature as Canadians apparently "appears" to us on our bank notes, the bank note imagery itself seems to "appear" through a conjuring act which is unfettered by accompanying explanations. The routes taken which lead to the specific images selected are not marked. The official literature does not discuss the process through which it is decided how Canada is portrayed, but states simply that Canada is portrayed. Clues to the nature of this portrayal, to the identity of this Canada, spring from the hope that a picture is indeed worth a thousand words and that an analysis of the Bank of Canada's bank note imagery from its first issue to the present will provide these clues.

The history of the Bank of Canada's control over note design begins in 1935 when it struggled for sole right to issue notes. Provincial governments and chartered banks had previously issued their own. The issue then, as now, was security and control and the newly founded Bank claimed to be better able to control counterfeiting. It set out to improve printing technology so that increasingly intricate designs could be issued to ensure its claim. The Bank of Canada pursues this endeavour to this day. Unlike the tradition of American paper currency which has not deviated from its "green-back," Canadian bank notes have undergone numerous design and imagery changes.

Through a self-propelled flurry of continuing improvement, set in motion by the initial rush to prove itself to angry provincial governments and banks, the Bank of Canada now claims to have arrived at the forefront of currency design. A line is devoted in each press release to the fact that counterfeiting is not a problem in Canada, nor has it been for years. Regardless, the Bank of Canada maintains a program of deterring counterfeiting.

The pursuit of the technologically more advanced note is the rationale behind the almost constant changes and plans to change our bank note design. An example of this can be seen in the creation of the new optical security device (OSD). According to a Bank of Canada press release of 1989, "Canadians can be justly proud of this technological breakthrough, which puts Canadian notes a good step ahead of advanced copying and printing techniques. Canada does not have a counterfeiting problem and the OSD will help to make sure it stays that way."

What "fascinating secret" might this aspect of bank note design tell us? The preoccupation it suggests with security, control and the law is met with the relentless pursuit of a technology that will ensure the maintenance of that preoccupation, in spite of the fact that there are no real threats or enemies to protect against. Compare this with the situation in the United States which have, according to a Currency Museum's employee, the most counterfeited currency in the world, and yet employ design technology equivalent to what ours was in 1935. Perhaps the American government is just less inclined to interrupt the cash flow of its spirited entrepreneurs, but more certainly it shows that country's own preoccupation with its history and the tradition of its "green-back."

Beginning with its first issue in 1935, which was issued in separate French and English versions, the images presented on both versions were as follows:

$2.00 bill: "Harvest allegory: Seated female with fruits of harvest."
$5.00 bill: "Electric Power allegory: Seated male with symbols of electricity."
$10.00 bill: "Transportation allegory: Mercury with ships, trains and planes."
$20.00 bill: "Toiler allegory: Kneeling male exhibiting the produce of the field to the Spirit of Agriculture."
$50.00 bill: "Modern Inventions allegory: Seated female with symbols of radio broadcasting."
$100.00 bill: "Commerce and Industry allegory: Seated male showing ship to child, harbour scene and blast furnace in background."

The same images were used on the following 1937 bilingual issue. When I first saw these images I was taken aback by how foreign they appear, lightly European but predominantly American. The promise, the optimism and the reassurance offered by the supernatural beings portrayed are not aspects of the nature of Canada as I understand it. Portrayed in these bank notes is what Gaile McGregor, in the *The Wacousta Syndrome: Explorations in Canadian Landscape*, describes as the American colonist's experience of the New World environment: "Under the influence of the millennial expectations of the 17th century, the early American colonist, borrowing concepts from scriptural explication, tended to interpret the empirical environment predominantly in terms of signs or types of supernatural events." Through this association, "the entire world became charged with cosmic significance and every human life was seen as part of a cosmic conflict between the forces of Good and Evil."

The landscapes in these images have been won over by Good.

The landscape is set in the distance and poses no threat, only the promise of space fully inhabitable and hospitable. It is almost completely obscured by the archetypal and supernatural figures which foreground and fill the frame. As allegories for the human domination and domestication of the New World, these images clearly present the wilderness as tamed.

In 1954, when the Bank of Canada issued its next series, it did so with the stated aim of creating "a Canadian dimension" through a complete change of these note images. Concerning the selection of the new images, the Bank of Canada stated only that "a prominent Canadian dimension was created by replacing the earlier allegorical figures with Canadian landscapes." They are described simply as a series of "realistic landscapes and seascapes."

Clearly the Bank of Canada felt that the previous imagery was not Canadian enough. The difference between the 1935 and the 1954 images is startling. The 1954 images are as follows:

$1.00 bill:	"Prairie View, Saskatchewan."
$2.00 bill:	"View of Upper Melbourne, Richmond, Quebec."
$5.00 bill:	"Otter Falls at Mile 996 of the Alaska Highway."
$10.00 bill:	"Mount Burgess, Alberta."
$20.00 bill:	"Laurentian Winter."
$50.00 bill:	"Atlantic Seashore."
$100.00 bill:	"Okanagan Lake, British Columbia."
$1000.00 bill:	"Anse St. Jean, Saguenay River, Quebec."

It is assumed, or hoped, that the Canadian dimension that these images create is self-apparent. How does this created dimension imagine itself and how do these images locate it? The allegory of garden paradise in the previous images is gone, replaced by realism. This realism is attained by beginning the image production process with a photograph of the landscape. The photograph is then used as the source for a painted image, a procedure also employed by many Canadian landscape painters from Tom Thompson to Jack Chambers. The painted step in the procedure, which brings in a "human" touch, is almost apologized for in the Currency Museum's display text: "Because of some of the technical and aesthetic considerations of Bank note design, the illustrations may vary slightly from the actual locations depicted." The engraving made from the painting renders it mechanically reproducible but so intricately detailed that it is as difficult to copy as possible. The resulting landscape has a technological aesthetic, a realism devoid of subjective interpretation or of the mythicized encounter with the landscape in the 1935 series. This process of demythicizing the landscape is also commented on by McGregor: "Too extensively demythicized the environment tends simply to become a kind of void that resists all human connection. This is what happens in Canada."

What evidence of this void can be found in the Canadian dimension series? Whereas all the previous issue images celebrated the inhabitable and benevolent landscape, only half of the 1954 series show any sign of a human presence at all and it is revealing to look at how this human presence is portrayed.

For example, the $1 bill presents the landscape as a vast expanse under a stormy sky. Cutting through it are telephone poles, a dirt road and a barbed wire fence that recede in one-point perspective to a distant grain elevator poised on the horizon. A large thunderhead hangs just above the tiny structure. It is a far and rather lonely cry from the Agriculture allegory seated in her throne surrounded by heaps of produce. The thin threads of transportation (road) and communication (poles) provide little reassurance against the distant storm and vast space.

The $2 bill shows three or four small farm houses and a church clustered in the centre of the mid-ground. The distant houses are alone and unreachable. The $1000 image is like the $2 one, showing a few structures in the mid-ground, but here the foreground is greatly reduced and mountains loom on the horizon which almost obscures the sky. The vast landscape again engulfs a few buildings. This image is also in stark contrast to its previous image of the Security allegory.

CHANGING IDENTITIES

The remaining images of the 1954 series depict landscapes devoid of human presence and of these only the $100 one has a foreground which it seems possible to enter. The other images do not suggest possible passage through them, their foregrounds blocked by rapids, trees or snow. The images on the $5, $10 and $20 bills specifically appear utterly wild and alien. McGregor suggests that, "The real relevance of the wilderness mythos to Canada can be seen only if we pay attention to what its proponents show us unconsciously, rather than giving too much weight to what they say they are doing."

What do the 1954 images show us, given that they are to create a dimension that is Canadian? With regard to the portrayal of Canadians within the Canadian landscape, they unquestionably show a great deal of It and a little of Us. We huddle together while the landscape surrounds us and look out at a wilderness that prohibits our entry. Northrop Frye has termed this response to the Canadian landscape the "garrison mentality" and McGregor has termed it the "Wacousta syndrome."

Between 1969 and 1975 a new set of images replaces the 1954 issue. They are as follows:

$1.00 bill:	"Parliament Hill across Ottawa River."
$2.00 bill:	"Inuit hunting scene on Baffin Island."
$5.00 bill:	"Salmon seine, Johnson Strait, Vancouver Island."
$10.00 bill:	"Polymer Corporation, Sarnia, Ontario."
$20.00 bill:	"Morraine Lake, Alberta."
$50.00 bill:	"Dome Formation, Royal Canadian Mounted Police, Musical Ride."
$100.00 bill:	"Waterfront scene at Lunenburg."

These images again provide an interesting set of comparisons. In this series the landscape becomes inhabitable again, but without the assistance of supernatural beings. Technology, government and the law are now featured and, with the exception of the image on the $20 bill (found within the confines of a National

Park), all these new images show clear signs of human presence.

In the new $10 bill this presence overwhelms the landscape: it presents a techno-scape where not a trace of Nature remains. This complete reversal is all the more remarkable because of the extremes it represents.

Into this new configuration of It and Us, a third term is introduced by the first appearance of Them in Bank of Canada notes. "They" are the Inuit pictured on the $2 bill, appearing in the harshest of the series landscapes. With minimal (low-tech) means, they interact with the icy environment in a nostalgic hunting scene. Nostalgia plays a part as well in the ship building industry pictured on the $100 bill with its sailing ships of a bygone era.

The government is presented on the $1 bill back and centre, crowning Parliament Hill and overlooking the river. The threatening storm and the vast distances portrayed on the previous $1 bill are replaced by an image of a log-choked river (prosperity through natural resources), overseen by government's central body. It is worth mentioning here that the industrial scene on the $10 bill of this series depicts Polymer Corp. which was at the time of issue a crown-owned company.

While the government is portrayed on the $1 bill centrally placed and looking outward from its vantage on the hilltop, the law is portrayed as a ring looking inward. The R.C.M.P. Dome Formation on the $50 bill gives the unfortunate impression of a law force poised to attack itself, its weapons pointed in. The threat of the sea presented in the previous $50 bill is replaced by an image which shows the national police force ceremonially closed in on itself in a circle with nothing at the centre save the threat of its own spear.

The idea of generalized landscapes re-emerges with the current series issue. The current series began in 1986 and the Bank of Canada's decision to make the change is described as follows: "There were three principal reasons for its introduction: technological advances in printing and photocopying of coloured graphic material that made the earlier series more vulnerable to counterfeiting; the need to facilitate the operation of high-speed, note-sorting machines by means of a bar code; and the development of features to assist the visually impaired." These new notes which come to be through "advanced Canadian technology" and make "le Canada a l'avant-garde de la conception des billets de banque" picture the Canadian landscape utterly devoid of any human presence. The word "CANADA" now fills the sky of a landscape solely inhabited by birds.

Buried under assurances that these new notes are even more secure and are more helpful than before, the question that lurks is "Where did We go?" Optical security devices, electronic readers and high speed note-sorting machines do not provide an answer. Perhaps the question is not a relevant one, the "predominantly Canadian dimension" being technology itself and not the imagistic concern of locating Us, Here.

The 1986 issue images are as follows:

$2.00 bill:	"Robin."
$5.00 bill:	"Belted Kingfisher."
$10.00 bill:	"Osprey."
$20.00 bill:	"Common Loon."
$50.00 bill:	"Snowy Owl."
$100.00 bill:	"Canada Goose."

The bird images are constructed so that they best accommodate the advanced security printing technology. The design criteria state, however, that specific birds were selected because they have wide nesting ranges and would therefore be most familiar to Canadians. There is a concern, then, for recognizability.

While the birds are specifically named, the landscapes are general; the wetlands, the grasslands, the northern wilderness. The specific locations of "here" in most of the previous images (Otter Falls at mile 996 on the Alaska Highway, Upper Melbourne, Richmond, etc.) are now replaced by a general image of "there." The placement of birds, large in the immediate foreground, right of centre and facing left, is done for reasons concerning printing and verifiability. The landscapes are minimal, primarily to contrast the detail in the birds, and for reasons of cost. Because of this, the birds seem separate from the landscape—momentarily halted, ready to fly off again.

The Canadian landscape here is seen as utterly uninhabitable and unenterable, the possibility of moving through it blocked by the apparition of its own name in huge block letters. The unconscious treatment of the landscape may be more familiar and more recognizable to Canadians than are the birds that fly in front of it. Looking out across a sparse and unlocatable land we see only the ghostly name of ourselves, a mirage which names our country but prohibits passage over its own horizon.

Sports

WHEN MORE CAMERAS COVER the Super Bowl than any major war; when, to cite one example, baseball's Alex Rodriguez signs a $250 million (U.S.) contract; when there seem to be as many jock-talk radio stations as there are "easy listening" spots on your dial; when there is a specialty television channel devoted solely to golf—it's time to read the cultural and social impact of sports. This is all the more important when one realizes that most sports coverage (on t.v., in print, on radio) is clichéd and/or vacuous (as in, "they oughta trade x, y and z for m, n and p"). Commentators rhapsodize over the beauty(?) of sports stadia, rue the athlete's inflated salaries and relate the insignificant status of sports vs. cataclysmic world events. Very seldom, though, does one encounter the kind of sustained critical inquiry that, say, one finds in a piece of literary criticism. With many more people consuming soccer's World Cup than Orwell's *Brave New World*, the need for investigation of the kind one finds in the following pages is significant.

GAMAL ABDEL-SHEHID,

"Raptor Morality: Blacks, Basketball and National Identity"

This essay examines concisely but intelligently issues of national identity, sport and race. Abdel-Shehid discusses not only the different ways hockey and basketball register on us Canadians, but also the different ways they make their impacts on white and black youths. His focus is the Toronto Raptors NBA franchise and its implications for what he calls "the political possibilities of Black public masculinity." For all the hype out there about Vince Carter and Raptor prowess, Abdel-Shehid offers some cautionary words and insightful analysis about the marketing of the Raptors and the discourse surrounding the team. The latter half of the essay concentrates on how this "Morality" especially affects Toronto's black male youths.

Questions:

1. What does "tough geography" (in the last paragraph of "Raptor Morality") mean? Does it have implications for you?
2. What is Abdel-Shehid's take on our national identity? How does basketball contest that definition?
3. What are the links between cricket and basketball that the author makes? To what ends?
4. Abdel-Shehid capitalizes "Black." Explain.
5. Can you think of other areas of what might be called the sociology of sport that deserve scrutiny?

In terms of the Canadian debate on sports and nation, writers and commentators aplenty have named hockey as *the* sport of the imagined community that is Canada. Both hockey and Canada, according to the tradition, involve "(white) Man's" persistent struggle against the elements, his attempt to carve out a home in the midst of a cold and hostile land.

It is thought that hockey represents the discernible difference between Canadians and "our" neighbours, the Americans. In terms of gender, a mythical Canadian heterosexual machismo is fashioned, according to Roy MacGregor, by virtue of fathers and sons playing shinny on the backyard rink and by moms and dads taking their boys across the country to play in tournaments with other Canadians. Hockey, in Don Cherry's eyes, replete with fighting, slashing and destruction, teaches Canadian boys how to beat up on anyone who is different, the "pansy" European players, as a way to establish "our" identity. There are other "important" Canadian sports, such as rowing, lacrosse and curling, but these exist on a tier second to hockey. There is, if you will, a third level (space?) of sports (basketball, track and field, boxing) in Canada. These sports, it could be argued, have only recently been on the medal podium in Canada because of their "colour." These "Black" sports, by virtue of the fact that they are played by "immigrants" or, more precisely, by people who "look like" immigrants, have largely been narrated as unCanadian sports.

What this means is that athletes who are accomplished in these sports are often seen as a threat to our Canadianness. Otherwise, their accomplishments are simply ignored. With respect to Black athletic accomplishments being ignored in these sports, note the following examples. First, witness the complaints made by members of Canada's 1996 Olympic gold medal-winning 4 × 100 mens' relay team. These complaints centred around the fact that, in spite of reaching the pinnacle of their sport, something deemed to be attractive to advertisers, the team received hardly any advertising revenue. Second, there has been a continuous migration of Black athletes, which mirrors the migration of other Black Canadian cultural producers, to the United States and/or England in search of more support and recognition.

In addition to such athletes being simply ignored, there is a tendency to see their athletic achievements as threats and thereby disruptive of the national sporting fabric. This is seen if we take a look at the "common-sense racist" understandings of basketball in recent years. In conjunction with basketball's recent boom in popularity, there have been corresponding attempts to demonize it, both officially and unofficially.

At the high school level, the meteoric rise in popularity of hoops in Toronto has been met with various attempts at repression.

For example, several school basketball programs have been shut down. Their principals cite basketball as a sport that is ungovernable. There have been unprecedented "violence in sports workshops" whereby educators and cops get together to try to target and "tame" basketball's "attitude." These workshops are all the more offensive given that hockey, with its legendary violence on and off the ice, has historically merited no such conferences. In addition, in 1995, the Toronto Board of Basketball officials passed a series of restrictive rules governing the conduct and dress of ballplayers, including such regulations as prohibiting players from wearing cut-off T-shirts to games and preventing players from bumping chests after a basket. Some high schools have gone so far as to ban the attendance of fans at basketball games owing to two incidents of violence at high school games in the city.

At the media level, there have been several articles on violence in basketball. Articles cite the rise of the NBA and the antics of superstars like Dennis Rodman as being a bad influence on young boys. In other cases, journalists such as Gare Joyce write about the good old days, before West Indians played basketball in Toronto, as being safe and friendly. Moreover, at the level of the Canadian National basketball team, Basketball Canada, in the winter of 1994, issued a report exonerating ex-coach Ken Shields of racism. In its justification, the authors of the report noted that the lack of Black ballplayers in Canada's national program was not due to racist practices or beliefs on the national team, but rather to black "inner-city" ballplayers being unable to adapt to "Canadian" standards of what basketball is like.

This, though, is not the whole story. Despite attempts to marginalize it, basketball is now a popular and big-time sport both in Toronto and its suburbs. The popularity of hoop cultural styles worn by young men and women, regardless of their colour, is evidence of this growth. All over the country young people wear Nike, Reebok and other paraphernalia that signify basketball culture. The popularity of basketball, as against historically dominant sports such as hockey or baseball, is confirmed by the fact Toronto's largest sporting spectacle of the past few years was not a hockey or baseball game; it was the Toronto Raptors–Chicago Bulls game on December 10, 1996 at Skydome. Also, Toronto is gaining notoriety on the world basketball map, as seen by the signing of Trinidadian-born Torontonian Jamaal Magloire by the high-profile University of Kentucky basketball program and the staging of the World Championship of Basketball in Toronto in 1994.

This growth is not without its tensions. Primarily, there is a tension around what kind of Black public masculinity is possible in Toronto. There has been a price to pay for the rise of popularity of hoops in Toronto. This price is a result of the negotiation of difference that informs basketball's movement from a marginal sport to the coolest game on the block. What I mean is that at the same time as the sport of basketball has taken off and is enjoying immense popularity in Toronto and beyond, we have seen a new discourse emerging around basketball and Black public masculinities which has replaced, or overlaid, what could be called indigenous forms of representation. This new discourse is what I am calling Raptor Morality. It is, in large part, a morality rooted in ritualistic, African-American bourgeois aesthetics and politics. It represents a hardening of the political possibilities of Black public masculinity.

What is crucial about the Raptor is that it acts as the neighbour, or border, to conventional representations of Blackness as trouble; the Raptor can be seen as allaying or responding to racist fears about "violent" Black masculinities. The public positioning of the Raptor as a border is revealing, since it accords with historical practices of simultaneously narrating Black subjects as both "noble savage and vengeful warrior."

The success and the institutional solidity of the Raptors point to another process that we need to pay attention to—a nation-building project, the familiar imperialistic variety known as Americanism. While it is clear that Blacks have been written out of the official text that is Canada, the Raptors represent the most successful attempt to date to write them in. However, the narration that the Raptors are involved in is that of a new Black nation. More to the point, it is American.

I want to suggest that paying attention to the bourgeois revolution of Blackness, embodied in the entrenchment of a certain class of Black folks in Canada and the United States, is crucial to understanding the success of the Raptors. We cannot simply read the Raptors' success as attributable to a wave of anti-racism.

To help place Raptor Morality within the narrative of Black capitalism, some of the work of Arjun Appadurai is suggestive, specifically his discussion of cricket in the former British Empire. In discussing the way that cricket became important to India, Appadurai suggests that the ability of colonized subjects in India to play the game of the colonizers affords a certain power. He writes:

> Transformed into a national process by the process of spectacle...cricket has become a matter of mass entertainment and *mobility* for some.

The Raptors' success is clearly wrapped up with young Black males identifying and performing the dream of "going south" both literally and figuratively. This process, of looking south, is the performance and repetition of a certain notion of identity, namely a bourgeois African-American version of Blackness. Thus, being a Raptor fan, for many, is to participate in an American way of seeing and understanding basketball and Blackness. It attests to a kind of mobility and a way of responding to the whiteness of Canada's official narrative. Appadurai notes:

> But because cricket, through the enormous convergence of state, media, and private-sector interests, has come to be identified with "India," with "Indian" skill, "Indian" guts, "Indian" team spirit, and "Indian" victories, the bodily pleasure that is at the core of the male viewing experience is simultaneously part of the *erotics of nationhood*....*the* erotic pleasure of watching cricket for Indian male subjects is the *pleasure of agency* in an imagined community, which in many other arenas is violently contested....

Appadurai's insights are helpful here, since they point to one of the ways that transborder sporting communities are made. More specifically, they point to how important capitalist forms of sporting spectacle are to questions of identity. It should not surprise us that this is equally true for white folks and Black folks. For Appadurai, initiation into the imagined sporting community is a bodily and erotic experience. If we substitute the word "Black" for "Indian" in the above quotation, we get a sense of how Raptor Morality works. In many representations, notions of skill, guts, and team spirit are presented by the Raptors as elements of Black style. Thus, the performance of Raptor Morality is a performance of Blackness, the same kind of Blackness or, more specifically, the same kind of sporting Black masculinity embodied in movies such as *Sunset Park, Boys in the Hood*, etc.

The immense popularity of NBA basketball throughout the world reveals the success of a bourgeois revolution of Black public masculinity. It suggests that the attempts by young brothers to perform Raptor Morality in gyms throughout the city is in part about power. The desire to be "like Mike" is, in the words of Appadurai, a desire to partake in the "erotics of (Black) nationhood." Yet, this imagined community is a very conservative one and presents a caricature of Black masculinity.

By virtue of Canadian fears about Blackness and Black presences within the national borders, it should perhaps come as no surprise that the kind of Blackness that would settle here would be a conservative one, which is reliant on a series of Americanized images about what Blackness is "really like." However, the possibility of an American version of Black masculinity settling in Toronto and the ease with which it is reproduced among Black fans in the city indicate the power of imperialistic notions of Blackness, which the Raptors are reproducing in their marketing of the team. The strength of the Raptors' success underscores the power that capitalist sporting institutions hold in the (re)formation of national identity, be it Black, white or otherwise. In the place of what Dionne Brand calls the "tough geography" that is Canada for many Black people, the Raptors provide the blacktop and the myth of the hoop dreamer (made memorable in the documentary film *Hoop Dreams*). In this regard, Raptor Morality is ruled by what James Baldwin called "a theology of terror." Concomitant with this myth is the conservatism displayed in such admonitions as "stay in school," "say no to drugs," etc. The Raptors (re)colour the national landscape by means of replacing one Americanism—the nightmare of the 'hood—with another—the hoop dream. In both cases, indigenous Canadian Black masculinities are supplanted, affirming official narratives which name the nation white. In addition, forms of political resistance, something indigenous to Black Canada if nowhere else, are circumscribed.

It is hard, therefore, to call the Raptors' arrival in Toronto something which helps to consolidate a "positive" Blackness on the city's sporting landscape.

MARY LOUISE ADAMS,

"So what's wrong with *wussy* sports?"

Here, Mary Louise Adams explores the intersection of sexuality and sport or, to be specific, masculinity and figure skating. She is interested in the way male figure skaters, in her words, attempt "to jump into line with a hegemonic [or uniform] masculinity." By studying the way the media and the Canadian Figure Skating Association wrote—and continue to write—about such leading Canadian male figure skaters as Kurt Browning and, more recently, Elvis Stojko, Adams gains a keen insight into the way masculinity is factored into their images. This, she feels, confers respectability on them in a heteronormative world; in addition, respectability is conferred on the sport of figure skating, making it easier for boys to enrol in figure skating programs.

Questions:

1. Do you like the title?
2. What research went into the writing of this article?
3. Again, as in the previous essay, there is a comparison between hockey and another sport—this time figure skating. Why?
4. Adams pays close attention to vocabulary in her piece. Discuss the importance of this line of investigation.
5. The last sentence reveals a sharply argumentative stance. Is that a good place for it?

I first noticed it about ten years ago—not on the ice but in an issue of *Saturday Night* magazine. After a childhood and adolescence spent immersed in figure skating, I had been away from the sport, as participant and spectator, for a number of years. I certainly wasn't prepared for an image of Kurt Browning, a figure skater, done up as the epitome of urban cool—cocky black beret, tight jeans, leather bomber jacket. The adjective used to describe him was "macho." I had never seen the words "macho" and "figure skating" in such close proximity.

Five years later, the "macho turn" in skating was well underway. In 1994, the *Globe and Mail* included Browning on its year-end list of the 25 most powerful personalities in Canadian sport. Not only had he won four world titles and landed the first quadruple jump in competition, apparently he'd also "wiped away the stereotype of effeminate male skaters."

Although the pronouncement was a bit premature, it is true that since Browning became world champion in 1989, male skaters have been taken more seriously. Browning, for instance, was the first male skater to land endorsement contracts with major corporations such as Toshiba and Coca-Cola. Elvis Stojko, who succeeded him, has long-term contracts with McCain's, McDonald's, Canon and Roots. Much of this commercial success comes from winning world championships. But Brian

Orser was also a world champion and no comparable endorsement contracts ever came his way, suggesting that there is more to gaining corporate support than medals.

Skating is being straightened up. The straighter it gets, the more marketable its skaters become. And, I suspect, the more marketable it becomes, the straighter are the skaters. To read the sports section of your daily newspaper it would seem that this is a great thing—finally male skaters are getting the respect they deserve. They are being taken seriously as athletes. No one snickers about Elvis Stojko.

How is it that yesterday's sissies are coming to be today's jocks? After Kurt Browning won his first world championship, University of Alberta sports sociologist Garry Smith claimed, rightly I think, that Browning, despite his success, would still not be considered a sports hero. It was mainly, said Smith, "because of the sport he's in. A lot of people think of it as more of an art form than a real sport. Skating is seen as kind of feminine, so to what extent can he really be a hero to guys?" This is the former life of men's figure skating in Canada, where the term "kind of feminine" used in relationship to men means kind of gay and where fear that they might be perceived as gay is still enough to keep many boys out of the sport.

Unlike their predecessors—Toller Cranston, Brian Pockar, Brian Orser—Browning and Stojko come across as real guys, fellows a sports writer can spend some time with. Certainly both men have been portrayed by the press as fitting easily into mainstream notions of heterosexual masculinity. Son of an Alberta rancher and trail guide, Browning's cowboy background was rarely left unmentioned by journalists and television commentators. He was presented as the boy-next-door, a gosh-gee kind of ladies' man, an athlete who, had he been bigger, might have had a shot at the NHL. Here clearly was a guy who challenged the notion that skating is for sissies.

While sports journalists appreciated Browning, Stojko makes them weak in the knees. He's the three-time world champion and, as of Nagano, a two-time Olympic silver medalist. Not an article is written about him that doesn't mention his black belt in karate; few overlook his fondness for dirt bikes. Stojko does the biggest tricks. He plays hurt. He does not point his toes (as Browning eventually learned to do). During the 1998 Olympic games he was widely and favourably quoted when he said, "I'm a powerful skater. I'm a masculine skater, not a feminine skater...! I don't skate feminine and I'm not going to be that way. I don't have a feminine side." Tough Guys: 2, Sissies: 0.

Stojko is, unquestionably, one of the best jumpers the sport has ever produced. But in the skating world he has been criticized over the years for the artistic quality of his programs: his often simple choreography, his tendency to take obvious rests, to telegraph his big jumps. In response to such criticisms, Stojko, his coach and supportive journalists suggest that skating judges just don't appreciate his overtly masculine style. The assumption behind the claim is that an effete "skating establishment" rewards effeminacy rather than athleticism, that Stojko is a misunderstood underdog who is simply being true to his nature as a man.

Some underdog with those three world championships and two Olympic medals. A recent issue of *Saturday Night* magazine—obviously a great champion of the new macho skating—included an article called "Skating is no wussy sport." Writer David Staples goes to fabulous lengths to construct Stojko as uniquely tough and masculine among skaters. Staples is probably the first writer ever to describe Stojko's American rival, the stiff and formal Todd Eldredge, as a "graceful" skater. The description helps Staples to maintain the tough guy vs. sissies comparison upon which he bases his argument.

Staples uses verbs like "sniff" and "natter" when citing skating officials. He finds it shocking that ties in skating are broken by artistic and not technical marks. He claims that skaters who have received artistic marks higher than Stojko's have simply been "boosted" by the judges—as if the artistic component to skating is merely incidental and has no value of its own. There's an assumption that looking "balletic"—being stretched, pointing your toes—is physically easy. And that comes, I think, from an assumption that the men who skate like that do it "naturally." That's just the way they are. They look like sissies because they are sissies. Staples, like others, writes of Stojko's rejection of dance training: "Determined not to look effeminate on the ice, [Stojko] refused to be a ballet dancer, polishing the air with sweeping arm movements." We learn that Stojko's dad thinks ballet is only for "ladies and Russians who [can't] skate."

In interviews, Stojko visits the same theme, as if that is what sets him apart from his competitors. In one pre-competition profile on CTV, Stojko says, "I was never into taking ballet. That's not me. That's not where I'm at. How can I say—Of course you can be powerful in ballet, but I try more to be the macho kind of guy. That's the way I am." That many male skaters do not take ballet is less important here than the way Stojko implicitly counterposes macho-ness with ballet and the way he suggests that the difference between them is somehow present within skaters themselves.

Constructing an opposition between athleticism and dance is a standard device of figure skating commentary. It is used as a means of distinguishing male skaters from female skaters and also as a means of distinguishing the various skaters within these events. In men's competitions, commentators talk about "showdowns" or, unbelievably, about "shootouts" between the "jumpers and the artists," as if one could not be both at the same time—a position belied by Ilia Kulik who landed a clean quad and took the gold medal in Nagano.

This athleticism/dance—or sport/art—opposition isn't only used to differentiate between skaters, it also structures the meaning of skating in relation to sports more generally. Could something that actually demands interpretive—i.e., artistic—skill really be a sport?

This is the question I hear under the defences of Stojko's artistry written by journalists such as Staples. If skating could just rid itself of expectations of expressiveness, if it could be less like dance, if it could evolve into a "jumping contest," then its position as a sport would be secure. There would cease to be a need to promote the virility of its male competitors.

In the past, skaters such as Toller Cranston, John Curry and Robin Cousins considered it the highest praise to be called artists. By contrast, many people currently involved in skating go to great lengths to play down its connection to art or dance in order to underline the definition of skating as sport. Australian sociologist R.W. Connell has argued that sport is the leading marker of masculinity in mass culture. It is assumed that masculinity can be forged through athleticism and that real jocks and real men are synonymous categories with no room in them for anything homosexual. Art, by contrast, is often assumed to pose a threat to masculinity. Hence, the overwhelming need to portray male figure skaters as athletes, as tough competitors, as anything but artists (which can lead to interesting contradictions in a sport that demands some level of artistry from its participants).

This emphasis on the athletic as a means of downplaying the de-masculinized image of the artist is something that also affects male dancers. But while dancers try to blur the boundaries between athletes and themselves, skaters and the people who represent skaters reinforce them, clinging to and augmenting, where possible, the definition of their performances as athletic.

There are a number of ways to do this: One can, for instance, talk about how hard skating is. A few years back, in a short documentary on CBC's Prime Time, Elvis Stojko complains that, "People don't realize that you come to the rink and you train everyday—you stumble, you fall. We don't have pads like hockey players do. We hurt ourselves pretty bad sometimes and it's a hard sport. That's all a part of it and I want to show a bit of that on the ice." As he speaks, viewers watch him falling and crashing into the boards.

Another way to shore up the athleticism of skating is to borrow vocabulary from other sports. Many a tired cliché has found a new, if ill-fitting, life in a skating context: "We [Stojko and coach] want to keep squeezing him [Browning] to get into an overtime situation and score." Verbs like crush, attack, overpower, gun, as in "gunning for a medal," are now common—despite their inappropriateness to the format of figure skating competitions—in coverage of men's (but not, of course, women's) skating.

Not surprisingly, the sport most commonly referenced by this jock talk is hockey. In Canada, hockey remains the definitive macho sport, the mark of a tough northern masculinity. Pat Burns, ex-coach of the Boston Bruins, has been quoted as saying, "An avowed homosexual, that would never be accepted in hockey—never....A wall would go up because it's a macho sport."

While hockey and figure skating both take place on the ice, it is hard to imagine two sports that are more different. Nevertheless, hockey impacts on the language of skating in a number of ways. As far back as 1970, the Department of Health and Welfare was using hockey as a reference to encourage boys into skating: "Figure skating is definitely for the "He-man" too. The amount of energy used in a full free-skating competitive program can easily equal that needed for a hard-played game of hockey. You need only watch the spectacular speed and agility of a top male skater to be convinced."

Hockey-talk about individual male skaters positions them closer to the centre of the sports world, closer to the centre of Canadian maleness—as if to say there is more to these boys than costumes and camel spins. A *Maclean's* article about Browning starts out by noting that "Until he was 15, Browning was a slick, high-scoring centre in minor hockey...." After the Lillehammer Olympics, Morningside's Peter Gzowski made sure to ask Browning, "Do you ever wonder what would have happened if you had stayed playing hockey? You're a clever hockey player." In *Chatelaine* Sandra Martin writes that Stojko "looks more like rookie of the year for the Toronto Maple Leafs than the king of figure skaters." On television Lloyd Eisler is profiled playing hockey—and getting injured while he scores a goal. It's hard to imagine similar talk or similar images of Brian Orser or Toller Cranston, of Josée Chouinard or Shae-Lynn Bourne.

In the skating world, the macho-ization of male skating is a hit. The Canadian Figure Skating Association says that enrollment of little boys in its skating programs has increased substantially over the last few years. Sponsorship of both the sport and individual athletes has increased and now comes from a broader range of companies. Coverage of skating in newspaper sports sections has improved in terms of both quantity and quality.

Some of this is, of course, related to the international success of Canadian men in figure skating. But it is also the case that sports journalists are more comfortable talking about skating when the guys they have to interview speak their language, when they revel in being jocks. One can only wonder how sports writers will cover the skating of rising star Emmanuel Sandhu whose image is more reminiscent of John Curry or Toller Cranston than of Elvis Stojko. Covering Sandhu, a former student of the National Ballet School of Canada, there will be no room for dissing the art side of the sport/art divide, there will be no way to establish his "guy quotient" by contrasting him to his arty competitors.

I worry about attempts to paint skating as a sport for guys, as an athletic rather than an artistic activity. In the past, skating was a place that permitted, indeed rewarded, certain kinds of "guyness." Skating (despite official CFSA assertions to the contrary) was a good place for sissy boys to express their own kind of masculinity. There are too few social sites where this remains a possibility.

In blurring the line between sport and art, skating also helped to blur the polarities related to a sport/art opposition, that is the lines between male and female and straight and gay. Male skaters, for a time, were able to reject the rigid gender dichotomies of the sporting world. Stojko and those who fawn over him will have none of this.

What I find especially unnerving and homophobic about moves to construct skating narrowly as sport is the way these moves are presented as progressive, as "the right thing," as if in discounting much of what makes skating unique, the macho-skating camp is finally getting male skaters the respect they deserve.

Elvis Stojko is portrayed as an underdog, a radical, for what are, in essence, attempts to jump into line with a hegemonic masculinity—the same hegemonic masculinity that has made it difficult for male skaters to get respect in the first place. To me this marks a closing down of possibilities for how men can use their bodies. It marks a small victory for the lowest-common denominator of guyness in a world that could benefit from a lot more effeminacy.

GEOFF PEVERE AND GREIG DYMOND,
excerpts

Mondo Canuck

Pevere and Dymond claim that the image Canadians have of themselves and the image others have of Canadians is a bland, dull one. They maintain that *Mondo Canuck* is an attempt to show that we're cool, man, that there's lots of pop cultural zip to us—past and present. Here are two excerpts, focused on hockey, that attempt to enliven who we are: the first gives a brief account of the guy who scored "The" goal. For those of you who can't identify either the guy or explain the circumstances of "The" goal, maybe Pevere and Dymond crash and burn because their emphasis on hockey itself reiterates clichés about us Canadians. The second vignette presents Don Cherry—probably the only person who still wears starched collars, or at least the most famous bearer of that veritable neck brace.

Questions:

1. Does capitalization of "TWELVE AND A HALF" work or is it too facile, too simplistic?
2. Similarly, do you like the words "hosers" and "dorky" or are they unnecessary? Are the authors trying too hard to seem "cool"?
3. The writers clearly want the following pieces to read in a light, breezy manner. They want to make Canadian pop culture sizzle. Do they succeed? If so, how do they achieve their ends?

4. Are references to Gordie Howe, Gordon Sinclair, Foster Hewitt and Stompin' Tom Connors apt or do they date *Mondo Canuck*?
5. What areas of current Canadian pop culture demand inclusion in a *Mondo Canuck 2*?

On July 10, 1969, ten million Canadians watched on TV as Neil Armstrong became the first man to walk on the moon. On September 28, 1972, TWELVE AND A HALF million Canadians tuned in to see Paul Henderson jam a last-minute rebound past Vladislav Tretiak. You've gotta love it: more hosers were interested in watching Hockey Night in Moscow than Armstrong's lunar leap for mankind.

But then again, it makes sense. Hockey and television are Canuck obsessions: mix the two of them together, throw in the red menace and a whopper of a national identity crisis, and you've got a potent ratings cocktail. Certainly, the '72 "Summit on Ice" was the most compelling soap opera ever screened in Canadian homes. For 27 days that September, we were glued to our sets, facing the abyss—well, at least the distinct possibility that Canada was no longer the world's supreme hockey power. And if we weren't the best hockey players on the planet, then who the hell were we?

Fortunately, we didn't have to answer that question. When a relatively obscure winger from the Toronto Maple Leafs scored with a mere 34 seconds remaining, our national implosion was put on hold (for a while, anyway). Of course, in a televisual instant, Paul Henderson's life changed forever. He was transformed into a pop icon: the national saviour who could skate. The mythology had us believe that he combined the best qualities of Gordie Howe, Stompin' Tom Connors and the Fathers of Confederation. In reality, Henderson was just a better-than-average player who happened to bang one in while twelve and a half million people were watching in schools, homes and workplaces across the country.

After the conquering hero returned to Canada, he had to hire a secretary to answer the deluge of fan mail. Henderson's endorsement opportunities went through the roof, and the federal Liberals—in the middle of a wobbly election campaign—pleaded with him to make a few appearances on their behalf. (The non-partisan hero politely declined.)

The rest of Henderson's hockey career was, to understate the case, anticlimactic. Within a few years of saving the country, our saviour was out of the NHL, playing in the hockey hotbed of Birmingham, Alabama. Today, a quarter century after the series, the Soviet Union doesn't exist, there are scads of Russians earning hard currency in the NHL and the term "Team Canada" now refers to a bunch of dorky-looking provincial premiers going overseas with the PM to try to attract international investors.

Times have changed, but Paul Henderson will never escape his indelible pop moment: it's in a state of perpetual replay. As he said in 1992, the twentieth anniversary of that seminal Canadian event, "Even today, no matter where I go, people want to thank me for scoring the Goal."

* * * * *

Don Cherry

Born: Kingston, Ontario, 1934. *Trademarks:* Thumbs-up gesture (single or double). Omnipresent English bull terrier "Blue." Sartorial trademarks abound, including three-and-a-half-inch starched white collars, impossibly loud plaid jackets and a variety of ties featuring either hockey-team logos or cartoon characters. Nickname "Grapes" derived from Cherry. Catchphrases: "Beauty," "not too shabby."

Broadcast History: After a long minor-hockey career yielded extremely modest financial rewards and only one game in the NHL, "Grapes" found a new lease on life as a coach with the Boston Bruins from 1974–1979. Cherry even won the Coach of the Year award in 1976, but ultimately found himself with the hapless Colorado Rockies in 1979–1980. His outspokenness cost him that job in the spring of 1980. That's when Ralph Mellanby, then the executive producer of *Hockey Night in Canada*, came calling. Mellanby, of course, realized that Cherry's characteristic bluntness (the ability to call a Swede a Swede) would make great television. The rest, as they say, is vintage Grapes. His four-and-a-half-minute intermission segment, "Coach's Corner" (with Ron MacLean as his foil, the sober voice of reason), has become a national institution, often enjoying higher ratings than the game itself. Cherry has marketed his brand of down 'n dirty Canuck booster-ism wisely with countless endorsements, a chain of bars called Don Cherry's Grapevine and his annual "Rock 'em Sock 'em" hockey-highlight videos.

Broadcast style: Beauty! Not afraid to go into the corners and mix it up, Cherry is an unabashed supporter of the tough Canadian players ("grinders") he loves so much. (Cherry has an almost pathological fixation on former seventies Boston Bruins John Wensink and Stan Jonathan.) He passionately believes that fighting belongs in hockey and holds pure disdain for "pinkos" in society and players from socialist Sweden, particularly cheap-shot artist Ulf Samuelsson. On occasion, his analysis stretches beyond the hockey arena and enters the political arena. During the Gulf War, Cherry went on a flag-waving tirade against those "wimps and creeps" who opposed Canada's participation. (If any other sports commentator appropriated the public airwaves to flog his/her political views, it would surely mean instant professional self-immolation. But the massively popular Cherry can get away with it.) He's a uniquely Canadian creation, combining the beer-loving hoser charm of the McKenzie Brothers, the right-wing curmudgeon quality of Gordon Sinclair and the genuine, hundred percent-proof hyper-nationalism of Stompin' Tom. Actually, the similarities between Grapes and the creator of "Bud the Spud" are telling: both Cherry and Connors have strong working-class constituencies, and a certain hip cachet with the university-age population. Both men are uncompromising, which elicits extreme reactions: you either love them or hate them, and neither Cherry nor Connors seems to care which one it is.

Ability to Pronounce French-Canadian Names: On a level with Foster Hewitt, perhaps even worse. Of course, Cherry's pronunciation of French-Canadian names is on an advanced Berlitz level compared to his muddy attempts at Swedish, Finnish, Czech or Russian monikers.

Instant Replay #1: "I'm trying to keep this country together. I'm the fucking glue that holds it together."

Colour Comment: As a certified Canadian pop-culture icon, Cherry is starting to attract academic interest. In 1995, University of Guelph professor Ric Knowles wrote a research paper called "Post 'Grapes,' Nuts and Flakes: Coach's Corner as Post-Colonial Performance." Knowles repeated the oft-heard claims that Cherry promotes "dangerous traits such as misogyny, homophobia and xenophobia, all in the name of Canadian patriotism." Knowles even had the gall to criticize Cherry's grammar! The cultural meaning of "Grapes" was also explored in a 1994 Sociology of Sport course at McMaster University. Perhaps one day a Canadian post-secondary institution will offer a full four-year degree in Don Cherry Studies. Sign us up!

Travel

IN A SPECIAL "NATIVE" ISSUE of *Borderlines*, Haunani Kay-Trask concludes her essay on the prostitution of Hawaiian society by asking her readers NOT to visit one of the world's most popular tourist destinations. Similarly, in *A Small Place*, Jamaica Kincaid, whose focus is Antigua, writes, "the tourist is an ugly human being." Despite these warnings, people, mainly from wealthy countries, flood so-called exotic locales. For the most part, the inhabitants of those locales respond, creating, producing and reproducing (over and over again) the spectacles that keep tourists coming back for more. Clearly, though, again in our "pomo" world, things have changed. Travellers—the kind who write incisive articles and books—have become quite self-conscious of what they're doing wherever they are doing it. Such awareness is subsumed in that kind of criticism called post-colonialism. Whites, males, missionaries, Americans, to name some frequent travellers, have had to become much more alert than previously to the implications of their trips.

PAUL WILLIAM ROBERTS,
excerpt

River in the Desert

A peek at the pyramids: this inspires the author to unfurl his prose, his mode of registering his wonder at, specifically, "The Great

CHANGING IDENTITIES

Pyramid of Cheops." Although this excerpt from Paul William Roberts's book *River in the Desert* begins a little snarkily—and dangerously perhaps—with some possibly uncalled for comments about "developing nations," it quickly becomes reverential. The remainder of the piece attempts to capture Roberts's awe. He sees, climbs and historicizes the "Great Pyramid." It gives him a frisson: "as I contemplated the astounding structure for the first time something made my bones tingle." Often written about before, the pyramids are a challenge for the author who wants his or her readers to see them freshly and to see that he or she saw them freshly.

Questions:

1. Is the following sentence an example of over-writing or of wondrous description? "If...architecture is frozen music, then Egypt contains some of the greatest symphonies in the world."
2. What about that problematic beginning?
3. What techniques does Roberts muster for his description of Cheops and his trek up and down it?
4. Does the bit about Napoleon add to or detract from the section?
5. How do Roberts's portraits of the Egyptians register on you, the reader?

Arriving in a "developing nation" is becoming increasingly hazardous. It's got something to do with the fact that "developing" is what the country would like to be doing, not what it is doing. Avoiding disintegration and utter ruin is an ambitious aspiration in over half of the countries on the planet these days. A "developing nation" is a far more ominous prospect than a "Third World country." Will it, you wonder, sitting in your airplane entertaining apocalyptic jet lag, have "developed" an airport, for instance?

Landing in Cairo is thus a very pleasant surprise. For a start, the *new* terminal looks like a giant suite in the Trump Tower. And instead of the brutal interrogations and muggings you usually endure at the hands of North American Customs and Immigration storm troopers, I was greeted with astounding courtesy, then ushered through a couple of brief formalities, and—scarcely ten minutes after landing—found myself seated in a snazzy limo hurtling off down a highway so modern I wondered if I'd flown to the future by mistake. It was a cool, starry night. Where were the crowded, boiling, dusty souks?

By midnight I had checked into room 715 at the Ramses Hilton, then the newest and tallest of all the new tall buildings in Cairo. I drew back the curtains, stepped out onto my balcony, and gazed down at the broad, dark expanse of Nile curving away beneath me. A vast skein of stars hung far above the river, diamond studs stuck in the shimmering black silk of night.

Across on Gezira, the Nile's island, ten thousand other lights twinkled. Down below, the Corniche hummed and hooted, teeming with cars and with people out to stroll or loiter in the cool breezes that mercifully float off the river even during the hottest months.

> Cairo is a vast city, the largest in Africa, with over fourteen million souls, each face evidence of a meeting place of worlds—Africa, Europe, Arabia, and Asia. It's a sort of cross between Paris and Bombay, glittering and grandly elegant at night, throbbing, chaotic, and sprawling by day. At dawn and dusk, those periods of mystery and transition, it can seem one of the most vibrant and exciting cities in the world.
>
> There is something curious about them, these famous pyramids, the more one looks at them, the bigger they become.
>
> Gustave Flaubert, letter from Egypt, 1849

One-thirty A.M. How can you sleep on the edge of wonder? No one else was. It was still Ramadan, the Muslim month of fasting, and the streets were thronged with people walking off the heavy meals that would have to see them through the next long day, until the sun once more set over the minarets and the muezzin announced that Allah would let them eat again.

The wide, dusty tree-lined boulevard that leads out of Cairo to the untidy suburb of Giza is quieter. Outside the Blow-Up Disco a few men in *gelabias* and turbans appear to be arguing but are only talking emphatically in Arabic—the Cairene form, a high-speed, guttural burst at maximum volume. There is a mist around the streetlamps as my taxi careers past stray camels and cars shrouded with cotton dustcovers. A sense of excitement builds.

"See, pyramids," the driver says, offering me a fifth Cleopatra Mild.

I don't see at first, squinting into yellow haze. Then I make out a massive familiar form in the distance, which melts back into the heavy gloom as we turn off the main drag and climb a smaller, winding road. The battered car, with its shaggy fake-fur dashboard and dangling worry beads, comes to an abrupt halt in a desolate spot alongside a colossal crumbling wall.

"Where are we?" I ask. The driver gestures with his hand at the dust and the rocks.

Warily I climb out, and, as I slam the creaking door behind me, realize the wall extends up into the night to an invisible point impossibly far above. *The Great Pyramid of Cheops.* The words themselves inspire awe. A man-made mountain of stone built four thousand years ago—perhaps more, perhaps *much* more—on a scale yet to be equaled. The sight of it sounds a chord in my heart, and I feel tears running down my cheeks. Nothing prepares you for the towering majesty of the last surviving Wonder of the ancient world. It looks designed to outlast every work of man that ever was or will be. Instantly it is clear why so many for so long have felt it must mean something. *Two and a half million stones, each with an average weight of two and a half tons....*But that is somehow not the point.

> For it is no easy task to realise, however imperfectly, the duration of six or seven thousand years; and the Great Pyramid,

which is supposed to have been some four thousand two hundred and odd years old at the time of the birth of Christ, is now in its seventh millennary....It was as if one had been snatched up for an instant to some vast height overlooking the plains of Time, and had seen the centuries mapped out beneath one's feet.

(Amelia B. Edwards, 1877)

If, as Goethe suggested, architecture is frozen music, then Egypt contains some of the greatest symphonies in the world: compositions of soaring genius that mirror the grandeur of the universe and its Creator. Like the great cathedrals of Europe or the religious complexes of the Maya or the Incas, these structures are gestures of the spirit, their continuing existence alone evidence of man's affinity with the Eternal—even in the soulless wastes of the close of the second millennium A.D.

From the dense shadows at the pyramid's base a bleary-eyed man in a tracksuit and a turban like a large bandage appears. "Country?" he asks. I tell him. "Canada Dry," he says. "No, it's wet," I reply. He shakes my hand warmly, adding, "Welcome, friend. You are welcome here." I thank him, wondering where all this is leading. "Pyramid," he explains, pointing up at it. I nod. "*Great* Pyramid," he then confides, patting a block of stone the size of my kitchen. "*Very* old." Again I thank him. "You, me, climb?" he inquires, looking up, up, a certain foxy challenge in his voice.

"I never realized how big it was" is all I can say, still wiping away tears.

"*Very* big," he assures me. "*Very* old."

At this point, as if on cue, two other, plumper men appear— his agents perhaps—and we negotiate. The fee for the proposed climb is initially steeper than the pyramid itself. "Special for *you*," the more roguish-looking of the two "agents" keeps telling me. "Special for *you*, not for *any* tourist peoples." A deal is finally struck—ten Egyptian pounds, about five dollars or so and a good day's wage in most of Egypt.

Seemingly content, the "agents" retreat back into the night, and I am left with my escort up the Great Pyramid of Cheops, Sayeed. With the agility of a mountain goat on Valium, he hauls himself up onto the first block in the southeast corner, beckoning me to follow.

We begin to climb. I soon feel like a mouse clambering up a gigantic ruined staircase, slithering through dust, seeking out convenient nooks and crannies, hoisting myself up toward the great dome of stars above this yellow-brick mountain.

The thing about a pyramid, when you're clinging to its side, is that its peak always looks about twenty feet away, even when it isn't—and it usually isn't. After fifty minutes or so, elation has given way to terminal exhaustion. My leg muscles are trembling in spasm, my heart is bouncing off my ribs like a mad caged bird, I'm gasping for breath and sweating profusely in the cool desert air. "Come," Sayeed keeps saying. "Come."

Finally we're on the summit, five hundred feet above the Giza plateau. I roll across the irregular surface, propping myself against the last great block. Sayeed smiles, offering me a cigarette. It's the last thing I want, gazing up at constellations, which seem unnaturally close and as hopelessly enigmatic as the symphony in rock fanning out in flawless symmetry beneath us. The apex of the pyramid is missing; it was believed by some to have been solid gold capped with some kind of precious stone. I stand where the eye sits upon the pyramid those Freemason founders placed so cryptically on the American dollar bill.

I am not the first person to climb the pyramid. I notice what Flaubert noticed, and wrote about: "One is irritated by the number of imbeciles' names written everywhere; on top of the Great Pyramid there is a certain Buffard, 79 rue Saint Martin, wallpaper manufacturer; in black letters; an English fan of Jenny Lind's has written her name." Weeks later I was to notice Rimbaud's graffito carved into the Temple of Luxor.

"I five childrens, me," Sayeed suddenly volunteers. "All strong." He rubs his belly, and I know what is required.

"*Shukron,*" I tell him—"Thank you"—handing over a little baksheesh, that mysterious extra all transactions in Egypt seem to need. The top of the Great Pyramid is a good place to ask for it; after all, we have to go back down.

The return journey is not the journey up. My legs are shot, muscles quivering uncontrollably at every step. When I look below—far, far below—it suddenly dawns on me how very dangerous all this is. One wrong step and I'll bounce from stone to stone all the way to the bottom. And that's a long way.

The fear is tangible—perhaps a price one must pay for trampling over unknown millennia of mystery. Dust, sweat, a pounding heart, lungs valiantly pumping. A step six feet down into utter blackness. A loose stone, my fingernails cracking as I clutch wildly for support. It seems much farther going down, eerily so. Flaubert was right. So was Florence Nightingale, that intrepid soul, who observed on her trip, also in the 1840s, that the pyramids looked "as if they would wear out the air, boring holes in it all day long."

I flop from the last stone onto flat rock—ground, sweet ground. Ushered by Sayeed into a hut like a small garden shed, I find more people within than I would have thought it could contain, all huddled around a sulfurous oil heater. Among them I notice Sayeed's "agents."

"All good men," the fattest and clearly most senior man announces, gesturing at the hunched forms with their disastrous teeth and hopeful smiles. Beyond him, through an unpaned window, an edge of the pyramid climbs at its faultless angle. Here are its current keepers, cringing at the sight of my camera, offering tea and cigarettes instead of initiation into the mysteries. What we have been doing is obviously not legal. It is hard to say which has decayed most over the centuries, mankind or the Great Pyramid of Cheops.

> It is truly a house of initiation in every sense, but that is not to say that the Great Pyramid was never used for anything else. Theodolite it may have been, astronomical observatory, in one sense or another, it almost certainly was. And there can scarcely be any doubt that pyramid-construction—even if not that of the Great Pyramid itself—lay at the very basis of

> the sudden rise of Egyptian civilisation in the third millennium B.C. Indeed, of all the various subsidiary theories proposed, only the long-familiar tombic, treasury and granary theories seem decidedly more likely.
>
> Peter Lemesurier, *The Great Pyramid Decoded*

Before the Battle of the Pyramids in 1798, Napoleon Bonaparte addressed his troops: "Soldiers, consider that from the summit of these pyramids, forty centuries look down upon you." Time itself, it was said, feared the pyramids. Originally encased in polished white limestone—which must have been a staggering sight, a vast gleaming crystal—the Great Pyramid has presided over Egypt for as long as we know, indifferent to every conqueror, indifferent to the long centuries themselves. It was already an ancient monument when the biblical Abraham visited Egypt, as the texts suggest he did; and it was still there when Napoleon defeated the Mamelukes in its shadow at the close of the eighteenth century.

Bringing with his army a team of scholars and scientists, Napoleon helped usher in the modern wave of interest in ancient Egypt that, much assisted by the discovery of Tutankhamen's tomb in the 1920s, has continued to the present day. Between the seventh century, when the Arabs who conquered Egypt in the name of Islam stripped the casing stones from the pyramids to build the mosques of Cairo, and the Renaissance, the monuments of Giza lay unnoticed beneath drifting sands at the desert's edge. It is hard to understand how. Perhaps their essential mystery and all that it still entails is an answer. What are they? What are they for? What do they mean?

The existence of the Giza pyramids is sheer effrontery, even to modern man. The reaction they elicit has often been hostility. Even Herodotus, writing five centuries before Christ about something as far away from his own time as we are from him, confidently proffers old and unsubstantiated gossip as truth.

Cheops' supposed ego has been a problem for many writers—as if the Great Pyramid were some ultimate macho threat. Such a bastard was this Cheops, according to Herodotus, that, short of cash for his ambitious building projects at one point, he made his daughter work as a prostitute to help him out. Upset but dutifully compliant, she asked of all her clients a further fee besides what she was expected to turn over to Dad—a block of stone with which to build her own pyramid. Hers still stands at the foot of her father's more substantial effort. Is the story true? Well, there are more than a hundred thousand blocks of stone in the pyramid associated with Cheops' daughter....

Like everything written about the Great Pyramid, nothing in Herodotus can be proven, though much can be disproven. As Peter Lemesurier points out in one of the most recent books on the subject, the most common assumption, that the pyramids were tombs, is the most easily disproven. Even Herodotus, the earliest historian to write about the Great Pyramid, records he was told categorically by the Egyptian priesthood that Cheops, or Khufu, as he's also called, was never buried in the pyramid at all. He was apparently interred on a secret, subterranean island beneath the waters of the Nile. If he'd wanted his tomb to avoid attention, you can't help but ask, why would he have constructed the largest building on earth to house it? If the body was never there, that might explain why the Arabs who broke into the pyramid's upper passageways some twelve centuries after Herodotus found that it *still* wasn't there. The sarcophagus was empty. This could mean that the mummified body had been removed, either for safekeeping or by robbers looking for precious objects often wrapped in the mummy shrouds. But Egyptian sarcophagi were often buried empty. In 1954, for example, an alabaster coffer was discovered in the tomb chamber of Sekhemket's unfinished pyramid at Saqqara; it had been carefully sealed, although it was found to be empty when opened. The same is true of the sarcophagus of Cheops' mother, Queen Hetepheress, discovered at Giza.

Some pyramids *were* tombs, but the Great Pyramid is very different from any other pyramid in Egypt. Even that first night, as I contemplated the astounding structure for the first time, something made my bones tingle. Thinking about the story of a king who died, of a corpse placed in a tomb whose door was sealed with stone, of a god whose body subsequently disappeared from the tomb without trace, I couldn't help but feel how uncannily similar it was to the tale told about a certain man from Galilee....

STAN FOGEL,

"The Marshalls: No Island Is an Island"

The Marshall Islands, famously, contain Bikini Atoll (interestingly named), a major U.S. testing area for nuclear weapons. They are also a tourist destination. The following article attempts to examine this seeming contradiction. In an era during which an increasing number of people are alert to the domination of one country by another or the domination of one group by another, "The Marshalls: No Island Is an Island" fits into the growing category of literature called post-colonial; "poco" (for short) works seek to read the legacy of this kind of occupation. The Marshalls present an unusually condensed version of "invasion" since they consist of atolls themselves comprising tiny islands; displacement there can be seen quite starkly.

Questions:

1. "Irony" is mentioned frequently in the following essay. Discuss its importance as an essay-writing technique.
2. What are the characteristics of a travel brochure? Why does Fogel debunk them?
3. What are the characteristics of travel literature? Does "The Marshalls: No Island Is an Island" fit the definition?
4. Do you like the last paragraph of the piece? Is the shift in focus from political to personal concerns a worthwhile tactic?
5. It has been said that contemporary travel writers are by and large middle-aged, middle-class white men from the so-called

first world. Do you feel that this is relevant to the consideration of travel literature?

It is easy to slip into a tropical paradise. You take a plane trip or you read some travel writing, such as the following: "Sit by the placid lagoon and you can hear the muted roar of waves spilling over the reef on the open ocean side of the atoll. Tranquil days on alabaster beaches, nights illuminated by the flicker of starlight on a glassy sea...." That is from Continental/Air Micronesia's brochure on the Marshall Islands, atolls laid out like a gigantic golf course in the mid-Pacific. The brochure's cover features the requisite Gauguinesque beauty, her smile, dark skin, the outline of a bare breast and an ocean backdrop all meant to be as readable, that is to say, as accessible and inviting as any pulp novel.

My initial landing on Majuro, capital of the Marshall Islands, was both as tropical and clichéd as one could want: descending the plane's rear steps, my thonged feet were immediately encased in snug-rich equatorial air that loosened my gait and relaxed me before I touched the ground.

You should also know (readers of travel writing being the most voyeuristic of consumers) of another idyllic vignette: of a stay on a "deserted" island two-thirds of the way along the Majuro Atoll. The Marshalls consist of a number of atolls each with a cluster of large and small islands (most of them uninhabited) connected by a reef that can be walked on during low tide. (The stroll provides a surrealistic experience as you walk between islands, towering Pacific waves breaking for no visible reason a few feet away.) Sleeping on a grass mat in a little hut on the lagoon side of the island, made cosy by a semicircle of coconut trees; getting sweet, mild water from a rain barrel; watching birds chase schools of fish over an ocean luxuriant with many shades of blue; wandering in reef boots (surely to become the new urban rage—they look like tires with toes)—these are elements of the exotic, or the exotic as it is sold to us, a

Club Med vacation without the chatter of an Allstate insurance agent from Topeka, Kansas. Listen for the sound of a coconut falling so that (neophyte who isn't intrepid enough to scale a tree for supper) you can crack a fresh one and suck and scrape the pith that winds up ersatz and hardened in your supermarket.

Lush prose I could feed you like breadfruit until this piece modulates into mood music for an afternoon nap (as you nestle in your longed-for hammock). The Marshall Islands, though, have a history, itself the undoing of any Eden. Given that history, there should be no lilt or lure to its prose. Language here should be no conduit to escapist reverie. Despite the irreverence for human life they will shortly catalogue, my sentences will, no doubt, arrive on these pages more or less polished and poised. The following news report culled from the Marshall Islands *Journal* (with an inimitable prose style) may, perhaps, begin to deflect us from idyllic projections. Vandals had broken into the South Pacific Island Airways' office and the next-door office of Ace International.

> Paper documents, obviously moved in haste from opened desk and file drawers littered the floor of Ace, along with some broken glass. A foul word describing the between the leg place of the vandal's mother suggested that perhaps the poor misguided individual was looking for a return to the womb. Unfortunately it was not found and so solace had to be taken by squatting foot-perched on the facilities' nearby toilet and attempting to target a bowel movement into the chasm. Unfortunately the aim was not quite as good as the recent Iraqui attempt on the U.S.S. *Stark*, and a telltale remnant of feces was evidenced on the seat. And so another Friday night in Majuro winds its way into history.

As colourful as this prose is, it is also oblivious to its own history: in another of the weekly issues of the *Journal,* a sportswriter referred to a softball team "nuking" its opponent. In this vein, two of Majuro's major districts are called Laura for Lauren Bacall and Rita for Rita Hayworth. The thundering irony of the latter is that the U.S. nuclear bomb triggered on Bikini Atoll—which displaced a good many people and rendered the island uninhabitable—had Hayworth's picture plastered on it. Displacing the indigenous peoples, the bomb stands more literally than it does for most other nations as the central moment in the history of the Marshalls. Not a singular occurrence, nuclear weapons have been detonated on the Marshalls a number of times, once in such a way that it produced substantial fallout on and extended medical and social problems for the Rongelap people (who inhabited an atoll near Bikini).

Other intrusions by foreign countries have reshaped the Marshalls less apocalyptically but just as certainly. World War II, to cite one brutal period, featured a tenacious occupation by the Japanese. Since then the U.S.A. has leased Kwajalein Atoll (which contains the world's largest lagoon); this has produced another shuffling, albeit a less dramatic one than the Bikini evacuation, of Marshallese unlucky enough to reside in a target area and to be part of geopolitical machinations. A curious (which has quickly leavened into normal) situation prevails as a result of the American-Marshallese relationship. Called the Compact of Free Association—a wonderful oxymoron—the arrangement allows the United States Army to use Kwajalein Atoll as its "catcher's mitt in the Pacific" (as it has been called). Intercontinental ballistic missiles (ICBMS) are launched from Vandenberg Air Force Base in Vandenberg, California, and tracked into the lagoon by sophisticated radar devices based on various islands on the atoll. Kwajalein, the eponymous and biggest island, functions as "command central" for the tracking and retrieval operation. Access to that island is controlled; via petitioning, however, and with academic and journalistic credentials, I was permitted a two-day, one-night stopover. Included was a tour and meeting with the base officials.

I then moved on to Ebeye, an island near Kwajalein on the atoll, which the *Village Voice* has called "the Calcutta of the Pacific." That Kwajalein, the military base-island, provides as close to the constructed ideal of a tropical paradise as one is likely to find on Kwajalein Atoll (or on any of the other atolls) surely taxes the definition of irony. Kwajalein prohibits all but official cars, bicycles being the main vehicular mode; Ebeye, on the other hand, only 78 acres, features a brigade of taxis that circle the island faster and with less variety than Edwin Moses circles a track. Kwajalein's beaches are clean, its parks plentiful, its pace meandering; Ebeye's beaches contain more garbage than T.S. Eliot's wasteland; the only fertility results in children (half of Ebeye's population is under 16). Ebeye feeds workers to Kwajalein the way Beverly Hills estates absorb their phalanx of maids and gardeners, shuttling them in for the day and dispatching them before dark. Yet as the briefing by USAKA's (U.S. Army Kwajalein Atoll has supplanted the more threatening Kwajalein Missile Range as the area's dominant brand name) publications officer outlined, U.S.–Marshall Island cooperation is contributing to change on Ebeye: a desalination plant has been built providing Ebeye with a reliable supply of fresh water; a causeway is planned to link Ebeye with islands close by, offering the dense population a chance to become somewhat less cluttered.

Undeniably, much Marshall Island capital accrues from the U.S. rental of Kwajalein Atoll. Also, relations between the Marshallese on Ebeye and the U.S. Army have become less strained than they were some years ago when protests ("sail-ins" and occupations) reflected the Marshallese disquiet with conditions on the atoll. There appears to be no broadly-based movement to oust the U.S. from its preeminent position on the Marshalls. Also, while cheeseburgers and Budweiser appear to have become the national food and drink of the Marshallese, Americanization is rife even in countries which don't depend on direct military financial intrusions for their sustenance.

Scepticism is the first response of a sentient outside observer when s/he hears missiles called RV (reentry vehicles—but linked indissociably in my mind with recreational vehicles). Yet some sentient inside observers, Marshallese men and women, see better material conditions for the Marshallese as a result of their allowing themselves to become "a national asset"—the motto of USAKA, deftly worded to avoid specifying which nation. Is the money worth the displacement that has occurred on Kwajalein Atoll? Is it worth the commitment to the testing of weapons that has wrought grievous harm for the Marshallese? Putting the question so starkly (the pun should raise the whole issue of American militarism) belies the protracted, intricate answers the Marshallese are drafting as they live with that money and the presence it has sanctioned and will continue to sanction. Phrased by the U.S. Military the assessment reads neatly, logically, purposefully: the week before I arrived an incoming RV (we all get used to such euphemisms) destroyed a power plant on one of the islands on Kwajalein Atoll. It fell, all were assured, well within the target area; the power plant was old and will be rebuilt in a more advantageous spot; no fatality has ever resulted from Kwajalein testing; Kwajalein lagoon is kept clean by divers who retrieve all large RV parts (the RV shattering on impact with water).

Phrased by an outsider such as me an assessment of the situation has a sociologist's colouration whether one's training is in that area or not. Father Hacker, a sturdy, calm Catholic priest who has overseen the building of churches and schools in his many years on the Marshalls, told me that a visitor to the islands thinks he can write a book about them after a few days, an article after a few weeks, etc. No person, no people (and here language's labyrinthine, complex dimensions are primary) gets to write his, her or its history directly, transparently or truly. Unfortunately perhaps for the Marshallese, their story, their history is even more contaminated than most, nuclear contamination being the most enduring, least easily purged variant. Father Hacker's cautionary comment is echoed by Raymond Carr who, in an essay in *The New York Review of Books*, recounts an encounter with the Western world of an Indian from Chiapas in Mexico whose village had been invaded by an occupying army of Harvard anthropologists. Why, he asked, did we hold our forks in our left hands and use a small spoon for salt? What was the significance of these trivia in our eating habits? A Marshallese wit, when asked about the contributions of the U.S. Peace Corps, said that the volunteers do three things during their stints: fish, speak the Marshallese language, make love to the Marshallese women. He felt he was already competent in those areas.

My own reading, which is to say this writing of the Marshalls, contaminates their (hi)story minimally, I hope. Despite the, perhaps, intrusive nature of proclamations by non-Marshallese, many people in the peace movement, especially, feel strongly the need to speak about and for the Marshallese. That the author of the piece you are reading is no island, Donne's truism, my interaction with the islands and its occupants proved in both comic and intimate ways. Sitting in a bar in Majuro, a native Marshallese woman asked me if I were Jewish. (I am.) It was startling to hear that question asked in that milieu, even more startling to hear her say how pleased she was by this circumstance, that it was good to have another Jew on the island, whereupon her husband, a Jewish lawyer from Minneapolis who worked in the Attorney General's Office of the Marshalls, regaled me with the story of a Passover seder on Majuro attended by three Marshallese women, their ten children and the three Jewish aliens who were their husbands or lovers (a scene, *pace* Roth, as far from the middle-class North American seder as the Marshall Islands are from our ambit).

There is also the story of my presence on the Marshalls: I was propelled there by a desire to be with someone who had research to do on the Marshalls. That story, too, is travel writing of a sort, but it contains, I would tentatively maintain, no injustices whatsoever.

KAREN CONNELLY,
excerpt

Touch the Dragon: A Thai Journal

Karen Connelly was only a teenager when she embarked upon a Rotary Club–sponsored year in Denchai, a small town in rural Thailand. The diary that she kept and, she says, honed for five years ultimately became *Touch the Dragon: A Thai Journal*. For that book Connelly won the 1993 Governor General's Award for Non-fiction, becoming the youngest English Canadian recipient of that award. In *Touch the Dragon* Connelly records with lyricism and youthfulness her impressions of Thai culture. One of her focuses represented here is women's lives in Thailand. Connelly's book, though, ranges widely over a variety of topics: food, festivities, her own follies.

Questions:

1. Note the metaphor in the opening sentence. Does it hint at Connelly being a prize-winning poet as well as a travel writer?
2. Gentleness, warmth: these are attributes of the excerpt, don't you think? How is that tone conveyed?
3. What advantages does the diary form confer? Is it a favoured mode of young writers?
4. What is Connelly's assessment of the living conditions of Thai women?
5. What other cultural differences between Canadians and Thais emerge from the brief excerpt?

February 16

SURAPONG THE LAWYER has enormous hands and a voice like the deepest part of a lake. Everything about him is oversized. He has to duck to go through some of his clients' doorways and he complains about the smallness of Japanese cars. "Whenever I drive anywhere," he says, "my knees go up my nose." Meh Dang is making a great farewell supper for him because he's leaving Prae to work for the provincial government of Chiang Rai. There are eight of us in the restaurant: Meh Dang (who is rushing in and out, talking, yelling, singing, carrying glasses and

167

plates, clattering in cupboards, forever a human hurricane), the doctors (who are discussing, as far as I can tell, bacteria, a nurse and the same old nasty administrator), the beautiful female interns (who are watching the doctors like little falcons but talking about the weather), Surapong and myself. All but the lawyer are drinking cold Chinese tea. He sips a serious glass of whisky. We are discussing women and he is teasing me.

"But this is why I live in Thailand, Kalen. It is too hot, I know, and the government is corrupt, but at least here the men still control the women!" The doctors laugh but Surapong's face barely changes. His eyes remain half closed, not in sleepiness but in cunning. He is great in an argument. "Pood lehn, Kalen, I joke with you. In the constitution of Thailand, men and women are equal."

I snort. "What's written down and what's lived are two different things."

"Yes, that is true." He takes a long pull on his drink and smacks his lips thoughtfully. "There is a good Thai proverb that says man is the front part of the elephant, woman the back part, the part that follows. You see, though, that the animal would not exist at all if one part were missing."

Surapong has perfected the Thai tendency of finding the pleasant and well wrought in any crooked edge. Perhaps his sense of fairness is warped because he is a lawyer. Meh Dang and her servant Gnop set the table noisily while we continue our discussion about women's liberation in Asia. Meh Dang is making more and more of a racket with the cutlery. Every time Surapong comes up with another proverb, Meh Dang almost breaks a plate. When he says, "Mai pen lai, Kalen, Thailand has come a long way. Thai men used to own their wives as soon as the two married. Now everything is different. Thailand is a modern nation," Meh Dang moans and bangs a dish down on the table.

She says, "Yes, very modern. Women pull logs up hills. People cannot read. A great country. No prostitutes."

The last comment is the only surprise. Surapong looks up at her, then down at the dish of food she's put on the table. "Ah! Very good!" he exclaims, "one of my favourites. Can you eat this, Kalen, or is it still too spicy for your foreign tongue?" And the moment is gone before I'm even sure it happened because everyone begins to talk at once in an orchestrated flush. Meh Dang swoops out to get the fried chicken, returns laughing and sits down. We eat supper talking and chewing bones, eating sticky rice with our fingers, burning our lips on hilltribe pastes of chili peppers, devouring bamboo shoots, baby corn, peas, spicy salads, fish and chicken, all of it variously spiced, boiled, fried, steamed. It is a great, long feast; as they empty, plates are piled on the neighbouring tables and crumpled little napkins sprout everywhere. We laugh as we always do, especially at the jokes about Ronald Reagan, but no one mentions anything about women again.

Meh Dang herself has joked about women in Asia, about Thailand's fame for prostitution. The silence comes only when people are serious. That silence bothers me more than anything else. They will joke, but they do not want to argue. The double standards are very frustrating. My guardians forbid me to be alone with Thai men, almost fall over if they see me wearing a pair of walking shorts, yet their houses are adorned with pictures of naked beauty queens and their weekends in Bangkok are full of frolicking in massage parlours. Admittedly, I don't know how *much* they frolic, but I'm guessing it's a fair amount. When Prasert took me to Bangkok last month to get my visa stamped, we went out for dinner to a famous nightclub with a group of his friends. After supper came dessert: a glassed-in room of bored beautiful women with numbers pinned on their long glittering dresses. They wear numbers, Prasert explained, because they don't want patrons to point. When each man had chosen his woman, they came wading through the pitch dark to our table, teetering on their heels, all shining hair and lipstick. I passed the evening with five Thai "dancers."

While we were dancing, one of them told me she would much rather go with women than with men. She kissed my cheek, which made the other girls laugh. She was eighteen and had been "dancing" for three years. When the music was slow and sticky, the men danced with the girls while I sat at the table eating decorative slices of pineapple and watermelon, squinting into the darkness. I was surprised. It seemed so normal, so typical a pastime for Thai businessmen.

I would like to think Surapong is not like this, because he has such a beautiful deep voice and is so intelligent, but Meh Dang tells me he has a favourite girl at the nightclub in Prae. "Why can't women do that?" she asks out loud when we are alone in the kitchen, talking about men. "If a woman takes a man who is not her husband, people spit her name in the street." She shakes her head wearily. For the first time it occurs to me that she may worry about Paw Teerug far away in Bangkok.

If I think about it too much, I get furious and want nothing more than to leave. It's a strange place. The chaste traditions end in red-lit rooms of numbered girls. In the house, Paw Sutape reigns supreme; when he has his tantrums, Meh Somjit cowers swollen-eyed and exhausted the next morning. In Thailand, it's a fact: women are weaker than men. The law may no longer exist, but in many ways, women are still owned here. Ajahn Champa told me about a Thai king of old whose power over his wife was so absolute that no other man could look at her. She went on a journey through the *klongs,* the inner-city waterways of the south, and when she reached her destination, her skiff overturned. The pregnant queen became entangled in water weeds and her own long dress. She drowned, surrounded by guards who could not help her because to look at her meant death. Ajahn Champa sighs about this, sometimes clicks her tongue and says, "Oh, Thailand." She herself could never be the hind part of an elephant. "I never married," she once said, "because my husband was never born."

February 19

WHEN I GO TO VISIT BEED at the service station, Samat tells me she's down at the house. Usually she works with her husband and the little girl, Poun, stays with the grandmother. I walk around the yellow guard dog, who is very pregnant and miserable these days. I'm sure she'd jump up and attack me if her belly were not so heavy. I make my way towards the old house through a maze of trees and bird cages. Beed's father collects birds: snow-winged, sea-green, red-headed rare parrots, macaws, Chinese-speaking mynahs. There is a blue bird with a long tail which makes me think of a giant paint-splattered magpie; there are yellow, orange, even green canaries, and a kaleidoscope of finches that flutter and sing all day. Some of them also sing at night. "My father does not sleep well without the birds," Beed once said.

The garden is hidden behind mossy fences from the clutter of Yantrakitkosol. A rain of sunlight spills into the courtyard and glistens in the clay water basins, where Beed's daughter stands with a cup in her hands, splashing water over her head. Unconscious of my presence, she continues to sing and toss water, hopping out of the way when it spills silver down the air.

I step into the yard and see Beed in the house, though at first I don't recognize her. Her hair is down and the tennis shorts have been replaced by a long wrap-skirt of orange and black paisley. I can't believe this is the same woman who changes oil and pumps gas and wears shorts in complete defiance of modesty. She pours cooking oil into a large wok now, humming to herself. The door is open to the kitchen where sauces and spices are piled on the shelves, filling several shoe boxes and baskets. Pots and pans hang on the walls; drying herbs dangle from the ceiling. Beed is working. The muscles in her forearms ripple steadily as she crushes cloves of garlic. Only when Poun calls her does she look up and see me.

"Ahh! Kalen! How are you? Where have you been? What are you doing with all those dirty feathers?" She comes into the garden with a boiled pig's leg in her arms. We sit down at the stone table and I tell her about my most recent letters from Canada and an argument I had with Ajahn Champa concerning proper behaviour for young foreigners. She tells me about a recent trip to Phitsanulok. Her voice unrolls like suede. She hoists the colossal pig's leg from her lap onto the table, laughs, wrinkles her nose, and begins pulling out wiry pig hairs with a pair of pincers. Poun comes to her with a butterfly caught in a bag. After cleaning the pig's leg, we make sweet Thai coffee and she roasts me some tiny "egg" bananas: they are my favourite Thai snack. Twilight slowly sifts emerald shadows into the garden, but we talk on about simple things, laughing sometimes, watching teak leaves sail down from the tired trees. I completely forget why I really came to see Beed: to rave about the inequality of women in Thailand.

She walks me through the garden when I leave. Poun trots behind us with her bag of butterflies. As I go up the steps, Beed says, "Be good for Ajahn Champa, Kalen. She was my teacher once, too, and she must be very tired by now, after so many students. And you are worse than most." She laughs. At the top of the stairs, we hear a low, sullen growl. "Be careful of that dog." Poun repeats her mother's words and waves her butterflies at me. "Come back next week to see the new birds Grandfather is bringing me from Chiang Mai." When I wave goodbye, the dog barks an ill-mannered farewell; the birds shrill and flutter as I leave.

February 23

THE MOST TROPICAL PLACE in Nareerat's domain is the library, a shadowy labyrinth of books, ferns and flowers. It is built of wood, yet entering it is like being lowered into a cool stone well; one looks around for the water and moss. I come here because people occasionally leave me alone if I hide myself among the bookshelves. I almost never read because there are too many things to browse through: old paintings of Thai kings and generals, teak sculptures of deer and elephants, a dusty collection of gems and tiny Buddhas. Sometimes sparrows come in the windows, shoot over our heads and careen through the doors, more audacious than the students would ever dare to be.

For the most part, the books here are too complicated or too simple, ranging from *The Life of Mozart* in black curls of Thai script to *The Adventures of Huckleberry Finn* in a simplified English version which I've already read twice. My study of the Thai alphabet is still limited to "Koon Suvit goes to the office every day" and "Noodles, fish and rice are delicious." Writing in Thai is like drawing snails and acrobatic sperm cells. All the letters are slips, curls, twists, back-flips. I've started skimming an old series of British encyclopaedias so as not to forget the English language. (When I reread my letters before sending them, I find very strange spelling mistakes and errors of syntax.) In the encyclopaedia, I browse through entries about foreign countries, insects and deep space. "The origin of all life is starlight," I read, and am deeply pleased.

I'm writing letters at an old table when I hear the girls. My first mistake is looking up and smiling. They come sliding towards me in stocking feet, each one a black-topped magnet. Gop, whose name means frog ("because I'm always jumping and eating," she explains), asks me why I write so much. "What, exactly, do you say?"

"I explain what it's like to live here."

"What's it like?"

"It's different from in Canada. It's hotter here, it's noisier, there are more people. The people here have cooler hearts, and laugh more easily. And I have to wear a uniform here, and watch out for snakes when I go for walks. No one skis here. Everyone eats lots of rice and som-tam."

"There's no som-tam in Canada?"

"And no durian, nojak fruit, no fresh pineapple sold on the street corner, no rambutan. No fish intestines, either."

They're genuinely dismayed. Poor Canadians! "You eat a lot of bread, don't you? And potatoes," says the chubby face beside Gop's. "And cheese, they eat cheese," someone else says, and the rest of them groan. Thais have a special aversion to foreign food, and the only cheese I've ever seen here has been that processed rubbery stuff which I believe they melt down and use to patch bike tires. Possibly the only thing the Western world has given Thailand in the way of culinary delicacies is chocolate cake. And a lot of Thais don't even like that.

Five or six scarves of black hair hang over my papers. They watch me write as if I'm performing magic. I must look the same when I watch them loop away in Thai. Gop, the group's spokesperson, asks, "But is there really that much here?" The other girls look around, trying to see what's so interesting in this cave of old books. "And who are you writing to?"

"My **mother**."

"Why?"

"Because if I didn't write to her and tell her everything, she would think I lived in a big jungle with monkeys, birds and wild men." They laugh at this absurdity, confident of their country's refined and gentle culture. Gop gazes at me. For a moment, she squints, not into my eyes, but somewhere below them; the other girls nudge each other in the ribs. There's something coming in all this. Suddenly Gop asks, "Is your nose plastic?" She is serious; the other girls grip the table and lean their chests into their knuckles like perched birds, waiting for my answer. I look at their low-bridged, round noses and touch my own, which is more defined, bigger, sharp. I explain that it is definitely not plastic.

"Then why do falangs have noses like that?"

In a hushed voice, I explain the differences between Thai and *falang* births. With the help of facial expressions and some complicated gestures, I demonstrate that Thais are born "straight," and come out face up, so their noses are squashed down on the way. *Falangs*, of course, suffer just the opposite deformity, and are born sideways, crookedly, so their noses get squeezed into a sharp point and set that way forever in the cold air after birth. The girls, all between the ages of eleven and fourteen, gaze at me with great black eyes, quite simply stunned. Apparently, no one has said anything about this in biology class. Gop whispers, "May I touch your nose?" I nod very solemnly. She bows in respect and apology before touching my face, that ever-so-holy part of the body. Her fingers are so soft I barely feel them. Every girl bows and touches my nose. One whispers, "But it really does feel like plastic!"

I laugh to myself. Gop is shrewd. She raises her eyebrows. "Why do you laugh?" I giggle. "What is so funny?" she asks. I still don't answer. She narrows her eyes. "Is it really true?"

"Is what really true?"

"That Thais and falangs are born differently." I make a hideous face and say, "This is what all falangs really look like." There is a murmured "No, no." "Yes, it's true," I say. "We only put our faces like this," I return my face to its normal features, "when we come to Thailand." They all shake their heads and refuse to believe such a lie. "And what's more," I continue, "is that not only are we born differently, we are not even born from the same place!" My voice is a little too loud for the library. "Falangs hatch from eggs! That's really why our noses are sharp! Our mothers are birds! This is a beak!" I say, taking hold of my nose. The girls whoop with laughter now because I've started flapping my arms.

"So falangs and Thais aren't born differently," Gop shouts, having figured me out.

"Of course not! We're all born the same way." She pokes me in the ribs and calls me a liar.

There is a sudden hush in which I find my voice caught, loud as a crow in a box. As always, I'm the last one to realize a teacher is on the hunt. I turn around with my mouth still open, spilling words, and see the librarian thumping towards us. She is old, hates noise, doesn't particularly like the children, either, and definitely is immune to foreign charm. Her thick glasses magnify the natural bulge of her eyeballs. She is an amphibious battle-axe, a two-legged toad with a croaky voice that orders us all out-of-the-library-this-minute-or-else-Ajahn-Champa-will-hear-about-this-you're-all-her-students-aren't-you? We skulk to the porch, shoulders shaking with bottled-in laughter. I'm afraid I'll burst open before I can find my shoes. (Shoes are mysterious things. Twice, I've had my shoes taken and been left with a smaller size in their place. I told Ajahn Champa I could avoid this problem by wearing cowboy boots to school, but she didn't think much of the idea.)

Literature

WHEN ROCKERS ARE LISTENED TO constantly, who has time for or cares about literature, you ask? From the evidence of enrolment in university and college literature courses, a good many! In addition, there's the freedom to produce ANYTHING in literature. While many of the writers in this volume (and elsewhere) take liberties with language (not to mention, their representations of life), in plays, poems and novels, a fiction writer, say, is much freer to write...anything and to draw on all the resources available to him or her. You name them—and you've no doubt studied them, so you CAN name them: metaphors, similes, alliteration—and you can find them inundating most literary texts. While literature per se isn't our focus here, we've chosen some Canadian writers who've contributed importantly to Canadian literature to write about...writing. They should know!

ERIC McCORMACK,

"Less than Meets the Eye"

Eric McCormack, a friend of ours, startled the literary world by producing *Inspecting the Vaults*, his first book—a collection of short stories—when in his late forties. He has gone on to be nominated for some significant literary prizes for the novels that followed *Inspecting the Vaults*. Clearly amused—and bemused—by his sudden literary fame, McCormack, in the article that follows, comments wryly on being a writer and being treated as an important one. He also treats humorously one of the key questions for literary theorists: where does the material for one's fiction, especially if it's gruesome material, come from? This essay is very readable and debunks many of the pretensions surrounding the creative process.

Questions:

1. "Telling truth is only possible when you don't know very much." This line is from McCormack's *The Mysterium*. What do you make of it?
2. The "author" is, in many ways, a creation of the media. Explain.
3. McCormack lists the essentials for "the craft of fiction." How many of them can be extended to the craft of writing generally?
4. Which statements in "Less than Meets the Eye" challenge your notions of literature, language and writing?
5. About violence in literature McCormack has some interesting things to say. What are they?

Becoming "an Author"

My first book, *Inspecting the Vaults*, was published in 1987 to my delight. Delight—with a price attached. After having lived a quiet life for so long, I was exposed, vulnerable as the proverbial bug after its rock is lifted away. A complete innocent (well, almost), I found myself on TV and radio shows like *The Journal* and *Morningside* being interrogated about the book as though it were the Holy Grail.

This exposure (in more than one sense) must be a sobering experience for any writer to go through. He fears at first he's the subject of some elaborate hoax. He can't believe his stories are being taken so seriously. When he realizes they are, he wants to say, "Wait a minute. There's less to them than meets the eye."

But that isn't good enough. His opinions on his own work, on other literary matters, indeed his opinions on *all human affairs* are suddenly treated with reverence. Gandhi-like, he tries to say only wonderful things. He varies his answers as much as possible, so as not to bore the viewer/listener/reader (with a mixture of pride and paranoia he assumes this omnivorous person will be watching, listening to, reading every single one of his interviews, comparing his answers, etc.). He exhausts his intellect, his imagination. He develops a nervous rash.

But some of his answers, thought up in panic, sound so convincing that he begins, cautiously at first, to repeat them. After a while, he almost comes to believe that he actually believes them.

Need I say this happened to me?

The Veteran

When my subsequent books, *The Paradise Motel* (1989) and *The Mysterium* (1992) appeared, my media persona kicked into action with less effort. No more nervous rash. I even began to relax and look around me a little. In the course of my travels in media land, I met fleetingly a number of the real stars—Margot Kidder of *Superman*, Terri Austin of *Knots Landing*, Peter Ustinov. I almost met the Queen of England. Meeting merely famous writers barely thrilled me any more.

On tour in Britain, my media persona, like any reliable incubus, did not desert me even on Auntie BBC—which, by the way, plies interviewees with white wine to make sure there will be none of that silence the electronic media abhor. In my case, they had nothing to fear. I merrily passed opinions on any and all matters I knew next to nothing about: on the art of composing background music for film, for example; or on why the Bolshoi Ballet was so superior as an ensemble to other European companies (inspired by the wine, I suggested this was probably the result of the dancers' all having been brought up in a regimented, communist society. The host of the show smiled benignly at that).

For a Scottish television series on writers, I visited two villages I'd lived in before leaving Scotland in 1966—they were now in ruins. I looked suitably distressed. But actually, I felt strangely gratified, like that Chinese emperor who wiped out all traces of history before his own reign. I hadn't quite escaped the ravages of time, however. During that same trip to Britain, I met people I hadn't seen in thirty years. We'd stare at each other in horror, each suspecting the other must recently have been stricken by a severe illness—until we realized the illness was only old age.

In interviews, I'd repeat my good answers quite shamelessly, melodramatically, as though I'd just thought of them on the spur of the moment. I didn't care any more about that hypothetical omnivorous viewer/listener/reader. "Get a life!" I'd have told him/her.

The Hard Question

From the retrospective shelter of my Waterloo rock again, I ask myself: What was it that was so phoney about all those answers to all those questions on both sides of the Atlantic? Why didn't I ever get around to saying anything that really convinced me? Was it because the transient nature of the entertainment media discouraged thoughtfulness? Was it because I didn't know what I believed? Or knew what I believed but didn't know how to articulate it? Or what?

Now I'm beginning to think that one important reason for my unsatisfactory answers lay in the very nature of the questions. After the usual inquiries about my private life, interviewers would almost invariably ask: What are your books about? Where do your weird characters and ideas come from? How did you develop your writing style? Why do you have so much violence and exoticism/eroticism in your work? How much of it is based on actual experience? What is your moral standpoint? And on and on, particularly about characters, and themes, and plots.

LITERATURE

These are provocative enough questions and I tried to answer them. I'd refer to the Border Ballads with their terseness and grim humour and I'd speculate on how they did or didn't influence me. I'd talk about the various little mining towns I'd lived in, and the miners I'd come to know; how tragedy, if it's repeated over and over again, becomes farce. I'd talk about the old Scottish schoolmistress who, whenever she turned her back to write on the blackboard, would terrify us by saying she was still watching us through an eye in the back of her head. And so on.

I'd go on for as long as the interview required.

Words

But for me, at least, this kind of concern was always on the periphery of what writing fiction is all about. Such things may indeed be important, but they didn't really seem very prominent in my mind during any of my confrontations with the blank page.

The fact of the matter is that my major, obsessive concern in writing was with words. With finding, or even being found by, just the right set of words.

"What is the relationship between you, McCormack, and these words that constitute these books?" Now there's a question that would have been nearer the mark. To say why the books were the way they were, I would have had to try to define myself, *tell everything that words could be trusted to tell*.

Too long for a talk show; too long for a life. You could spend what was left of your waking life trying vainly to find the right words for any one of the significant moments in your life. And who (aside from your analyst) would be interested in them? So much effort for so little return. Even that incorrigible hypothetical reader/listener/viewer would surely admit, "He was right. I must go and get a life."

And even if a writer were to expend all that effort remembering, disentangling, reconstructing, he wouldn't necessarily want to make it the subject of his writing. I certainly would find the exercise very boring, even though, from what I can tell, my life isn't that much more boring than many others'.

My motto is: Make things up!

Learning to Write

Now doesn't that last segment sound just like the kind of pompous "mystification" of writing that drives a lot of people up the wall? It's hard not to be pompous when you're talking about your own work and theories on writing.

Let me, however, be more concrete. "The craft of fiction" can be learnt. It's not easy, but I believe (I think I believe!) it can be done. Here are some of the requirements for the programme: (1) a hyper-sensitivity to words (2) a lifelong and varied programme of reading (3) a habit of observing and listening and imagining (4) a zest for living (5) a compulsive interest in dreams (6) a temperament that requires its possessor to write.

And there may be other elements—indefinable others. It's best not to think about them.

Reading

Writers surely ought to read more than just fiction and poetry. In spite of the current anti-intellectual trend, they surely ought to be aware of the major movements in the thought of their era. I refuse to believe that familiarity with the ideas of controversial theorists like Derrida, or Lacan, or Foucault, or Barthes, or Kristeva, or Gass, or Geertz is dangerous to writers, or will destroy their creativity. *Quite the contrary.* Look how much mileage this century's earlier writers have extracted from Freud and Jung and Sartre and Camus.

Our present-day theorists have given us a challenging approach to the world ("text," they call it) we all inhabit. Granted, their jargon is at times as forbidding as battlements. But within lie jewels.

To cut oneself off from today's most insightful ideas, to refuse to confront them and adapt them, is intellectual and artistic suicide. The experience of dealing with new ideas is as disturbing to writers as to anyone else. Which is why John Hawkes may have been onto something when he said, "The true enemies of fiction are character, plot, and theme."

Dreaming

It's a truism (but is it true?) that we should write about what we know. "What we know" covers more than just domestic relations, working in a university, or factory. The world of dreams is perhaps the most unique part of our individual experience. Convincingly to transform into language the primarily visual imagery of a dream is a challenging undertaking for any writer.

But it may not be wise. The sensible individual may decide to leave his nightmares alone (several of Freud's principal disciples killed themselves after delving into their unconsciousness), not drag them out into the day, embody the disembodied in words. I think, however, that's a risk writers must be willing to take.

Mistrust

The basis of one of my stories, "Sad Stories in Patagonia," was a particularly gruesome nightmare about a doctor who cut up his wife and implanted parts of her in his four children. I also made that story the root of my first novel, *The Paradise Motel:* What would happen to the children as they grew older, the victims of such a ghastly act?

It was a weird book to write and it was written in odd places; some of it in the Yucatan jungle (where I caught dengue fever) and some of it in the McDonald's parking lot in Dundas, Ontario (where indigestion caught me). In the course of the writing, I often had that feeling of being led by the words rather than vice-versa. In fact, the subject of language came up again and again in the novel. One character compared words to gallstones making their painful but inevitable exit.

A reviewer of the book remarked that anyone who mistrusted words as much as I did should quit writing.

I was a bit startled by that. What's wrong with writers mistrusting words? I believe, in fact, that *all good writing begins with the mistrust of words.* A writer must be careful not to be too susceptible, too romantically attached to words, too neglectful of their darker side, of their limitations. He must not let the words get away with murder.

Violence

When asked about the violent element in some of my writing, I would explain that much of my growing-up took place in the slum suburbs around Glasgow. Fighting and maiming and drunken brawling were commonplace. Coming home at night from Glasgow University, I had to hide my books under my coat; their possession would have marked me as effete, a snob who was entitled to a beating. This dangerous atmosphere was generated, no doubt, by massive hereditary unemployment in some parts of the West of Scotland, punctuated by brief periods of official warfare. During the latter, most of the young men joined the army. Their "peace-time" existence had been the best possible training.

That aura of violence can also be attributed to the traditional, omnipresent hostility between Protestants and Catholics in Scotland. It was a well-respected pretext for head-bangings and stabbings.

What about language, however? What about the violence in the Great Books that were used to educate us, particularly the Bible?

"I will destroy man whom I have created from the face of the earth...they shall be put to death, being filled with all unrighteousness, fornication, wickedness, covetousness, maliciousness, full of envy, debate, deceit, malignity...they which commit such things are worthy of death. I shall slaughter them all like doves of the valleys each for his sin...kill and exterminate them all, etc., etc., etc."

Dare we believe that such language has no effect on the

psyches of those subjected to it? Even in Scottish humour, the self-righteous zest for vengeance is prominent.

Preacher: There will be weeping and gnashing of teeth.

Member of the congregation (hopefully): What if you don't have any teeth?

Preacher (exultant): Teeth will be provided!

The Exotic/Erotic

I would rationalize these elements by suggesting that, like many other Scots, I envied R.L. Stevenson his self-imposed exile (for health reasons) in Western Samoa. I did, in fact, live for a year on the coast of the Coral Sea, in Queensland, Australia, and spent a protracted spell in the Yucatan. I couldn't understand those who didn't wish to escape (for mental-health reasons) from an essentially bleak existence to a more colourful part of the world.

But again, words, with their exotic and erotic aspects, must take their share of the blame. Any student of literature knows that even Puritan writers like Spenser and Milton were profoundly conscious of the sensual side of language. In spite of themselves, they couldn't help succumbing.

Mystery

My second novel, *The Mysterium*, was founded upon the word "mystery" itself—an ancient, complex word that has come to mean, among other things: "mystery" in the religious sense; "mystery" as the "mastery" of a trade, or art and "mystery" as in a detective story. The novel is set in a country that isn't quite Scotland, but something approximating it, amid blunt hills and mists, like those of the Southern Uplands, where I lived for a time.

The book concerns the apparent link between the mass deaths of the townspeople of Carrick (a small town among the hills) and the murder, many years before, of the prisoners at a POW camp that once stood near the town (such camps were common in my childhood during WW2). The mystery involved a consideration of such matters as hereditary codes of vengeance—some of those old Scottish villages existed when the Romans were building Hadrian's Wall—and mass-murder (amusingly, as I was working on the book, the CBC invited me to take part in a discussion on the recent glut of literary psychopaths; I misunderstood and thought I was to talk about "cycling-paths").

I liked the idea of having a detective at the centre of the book, perhaps because I sometimes think of the writer as a kind of detective of the unconscious (he gains access through words). I'd once written a short story, "Eckhardt at a Window," in which a detective stumbles upon a mystery that seems to have been created especially for him. In *The Mysterium*, I resorted to that idea again (I like borrowing from myself). The investigator this time was a man called Reeve Blair, who seems to be particularly astute.

This always puzzles and delights—how a book can produce a character who is much more intelligent than the writer himself is. It's part of the mystery of writing fiction, and probably insoluble, ultimately.

The townspeople of Carrick, as I've said, all die from a strange illness—or maybe a poison—whose major symptom is garrulousness. I'm not sure where I got this idea from, but it could have something to do with the fact that *all* literary characters are, in one sense, a composite of words. Over the course of many drafts of a novel, the writer dreams up, or eliminates, characters as necessary. *To be a writer is to be an assassin as well as a creator.*

Plot plays an important part in *The Mysterium*, not because I'm deeply in love with plot (though I don't mind it quite as much as the Scottish novelist, Jeff Torrington, who says: "I'd rather run my eyeballs along a barbed wire fence than read a plotty novel."). But a mystery novel needs plot—or, at least, the *appearance* of a plot. A very different thing.

In Progress (Process)

Last year, I gave up on a novel-in-progress. For the first time I had consciously done a lot of research for a piece of fiction, instead of relying almost entirely on the imagination. This time, I studied up the facts, took copious notes. In vain. It didn't work for me. Ultimately I was so weighed down with information, I became bored with the prospect of writing the novel. The whole thing reminded me of confronting a term-paper.

Anyway, I abandoned it. Maybe somewhere along the way, when I've forgotten all those facts, I'll be able to write the book.

I'm working on another novel right now which I won't talk about. I'm afraid it may be true that if you talk about the thing you're working on, you dissipate the energy you need to write it. That you should never turn the novel in your head into a dinner-table anecdote, because the words may turn against you when you sit down to write. "You've given us away too cheaply," they may say, "so now we won't co-operate any more."

All I will say about the work-in-process at this point is that it's quite exhilarating and quite scary. For me that's a good sign. Not that I'm writing for hours every day. But something is fermenting inside my skull. I'm not at all sure where it will end up, whether it will end up. That may be what's scary, in part.

Endings

As I look back over these pages, I see that if I'd started writing from another angle, with another set of words, I would surely have come up with another set of theories. I might have begun: In the womb, we lived in silent bliss; our first sounds were howls at our expulsion into the harsh world; words are the sophisticated expressions of the pain of that separation, as much as anything else.

Who knows where that might have led? But it would, in my mind at least, have been no more and no less truthful. Ah well, no matter. As one of those dying townspeople in Carrick pointed out: "Telling truth is only possible when you don't know very much."

CHANGING IDENTITIES

MAVIS GALLANT,
Introduction from

The Selected Stories of Mavis Gallant

Mavis Gallant, one of Canada's—and the world's—premier story writers, here takes on one of the great challenges of fiction-making: explaining why and how one writes stories. Less breezily than McCormack she tenaciously explores the will to write. (Some people simply—or complexly—*need* to write.) This piece is a sophisticated, extended discussion of Gallant's creative process. The care and thought that she writes about evidently went into the making of this introduction, which is as rich as Gallant's enriching stories. In it you will also find a wonderfully compressed memoir—of her youth and her decision to sacrifice everything in order to become a writer.

Questions:

1. "The distinction between journalism and fiction is the difference between within and without." Discuss.
2. Does the account of her young life reveal Gallant's future vocation…or does her authorship remain simply an act of will?
3. "Poised" seems to be a good characterization of Gallant's prose. Do you agree? If so, how does she achieve that quality?
4. Another aspect of the essay is the French/English divide. What relevance does it have here?
5. Both McCormack and Gallant emphasize the importance for writers of reading. What do you read?

Samuel Beckett, answering a hopeless question from a Paris newspaper—"Why do you write?"—said it was all he was good for: "Bon qu'a ça." Georges Bernanos said that writing was like rowing a boat out to sea: The shoreline disappears, it is too late to turn back, and the rower becomes a galley slave. When Colette was seventy-five and crippled with arthritis she said that now, at last, she could write anything she wanted without having to count on what it would bring in. Marguerite Yourcenar said that if she had inherited the estate left by her mother and then gambled away by her father, she might never have written another word. Jean-Paul Sartre said that writing is an end in itself. (I was twenty-two and working on a newspaper in Montreal when I interviewed him. I had not asked him the *why* of the matter but the *what.*) The Polish poet Aleksander Wat told me that it was like the story of the camel and the Bedouin; in the end, the camel takes over. So that was the writing life: an insistent camel.

I have been writing or just thinking about things to write since I was a child. I invented rhymes and stories when I could not get to sleep and in the morning when I was told it was too early to get up, and I uttered dialogue for a large colony of paper dolls. Once, I was astonished to hear my mother say, "Oh, she talks to herself all the time." I had not realized that that kind of speech could be overheard, and, of course, I was not talking but supplying a voice. If I pin it down as an adult calling, I have lived in writing, like a spoonful of water in a river, for more than forty-five years. (If I add the six years I spent on a weekly newspaper—*The Standard,* dead and buried now—it comes to more than fifty. At that time, at home, I was steadily filling an old picnic hamper with notebooks and manuscripts. The distinction between journalism and fiction is the difference between without and within. Journalism recounts as exactly and economically as possible the weather in the street; fiction takes no notice of that particular weather but brings to life a distillation of all weathers, a climate of the mind. Which is not to say it need not be exact and economical: It is precision of a different order.)

I still do not know what impels anyone sound of mind to leave dry land and spend a lifetime describing people who do not exist. If it is child's play, an extension of make-believe something one is frequently assured by persons who write about writing, how to account for the overriding wish to do that, just that, only that, and consider it as rational an occupation as riding a racing bike over the Alps? Perhaps the cultural attaché at a Canadian embassy who said to me, "Yes, but what do you really do?" was expressing an adult opinion. Perhaps a writer is, in fact, a child in disguise, with a child's lucid view of grown-ups, accurate as to atmosphere, improvising when it tries to make sense of adult behaviour. Peter Quennell, imagining Shakespeare, which means imagining the inexplicable, says that Shakespeare heard the secret summons and was sent along his proper path. The secret summons, the proper path, are what saints and geniuses hold in common. So do great writers, the semi-great, the good, the lesser, the dogged, the trudgers, and the merely anxious. All will discover that Paradise (everybody's future) is crisscrossed with hedges. Looking across a hedge to the green place where genius is consigned, we shall see them assembled, waiting to receive a corrective reward if only they will agree on the source of the summons and the start of the proper path. The choir of voices floating back above the hedge probably will be singing, "Bon qu'a ça," for want of knowing.

Janet Flanner, a great journalist of the age, *The New Yorker* correspondent in Paris for half a century, when on the brink of her eighties said she would rather have been a writer of fiction. The need to make a living, the common lot, had kept her from leaving something she did brilliantly and setting off for, perhaps, nowhere. She had published fiction, but not much and not satisfactorily. Now she believed her desire to write had been greater than her talent. Something was missing. My father, who was younger than Janet Flanner and who died in his early thirties, never thought of himself as anything but a painter. It may have been just as well—for him—that he did not go on to discover that he could never have been more than a dedicated amateur. He did not try to fail: in a sense, he never started out, except along the path of some firm ideal concerning life and art. The ideality required displacement; he went from England to Canada. His friends would recall him as levelheaded. No one ever heard him say that he had hoped for this or regretted that. His persona as an artist was so matter-of-fact, so taken for granted, so fully accepted by other people, that it was years until I understood what should have been obvious: He also had worked and gone to an office, before he became too ill to work at anything.

"What did you imagine you lived on?" said the family friend who had just let me know that my father was, after all, like most other people. He was with a firm that imported massive office furnishings of heavy wood and employed Englishmen. Not every business wanted Englishmen. They had a reputation for criticizing Canada and failing to pull their weight. Quite often they just filled posts where they could do no real harm or held generic job titles. It created a small inflation of inspectors, controllers, estimators, managers, assistants, counselors, and vice-presidents. Some hung on to military rank from World War I and went about as captains and majors. This minor imperial sham survived into the 1930s, when the Depression caved in on jobs and pseudo-jobs alike.

At eighteen I went to look at the office building, which was a grey stone house on Beaver Hall Hill. I remembered having been taken there, wearing my convent-school uniform of black serge with a clerical collar, and being introduced to a man with an English accent. My father was inclined to show me off, and I was used to it. What I had retained of the visit (or so it came back) was a glowing lampshade made of green glass and a polished desk of some dark wood and a shadowy room, a winter room. It was on Beaver Hall Hill, around the same time, that another stranger stopped me in the street because I looked so startlingly like my late father. The possibility of a grown daughter cannot have been uppermost: I had vanished from Montreal at ten and come back on my own. The legal age for making such decisions was twenty-one: I had made it at eighteen and hoped no one would notice. A few people in Montreal believed I had died. It was a rumour, a floating story with no setting or plot, and it had ceased to affect anyone, by now, except for a family of French Canadians who had been offering prayers every year on my birthday.

Years later, in a town called Chateauguay, I would hear a trailing echo of the report. We had spent summers there and, once, two whole winters. The paralyzing winter wind blowing from the Chateauguay River was supposed to be restorative for the frail. My mother, who never had a cold, breathed it in and said, sincerely, "Isn't it glorious!" I came back to Chateauguay fifty years after taking the Montreal train for the last time, across the bridge, over the river. I came with a television crew from Toronto. We were looking at places where I had been as a child. At one address in Montreal we had found a bank. My first school had become a vacant lot. The small building where I had rented my first independent apartment, installed my own furniture, filled shelves with books and political pamphlets (as many as possible of them banned in Quebec), hung pictures, bought inch by inch from Montreal painters, then a flourishing school, was now a students' residence, run-down, sagging, neglected. I would never have returned alone to Chateauguay. It was the last place where we had lived as a family. When my father died, I was told he had gone to England and would be back before long, and I had believed it. A television unit is composed of strangers, largely indifferent, intent on getting the assignment over and a flight home. Their indifference was what I needed: a thick glass wall against the effects of memory.

I drew a map of the place—town, river, bridge, railway station, Catholic church, Anglican church, Protestant school, houses along a road facing the river, even candy store—and gave it to the producer. Everything was exact, except perhaps the Protestant school, which we forgot to look for. I saw the remembered house, still standing, though greatly altered. The candy store had been turned into a ramshackle coffee shop with a couple of pool tables, the Duranseau farm replaced by a sign, RUE DURANSEAU, indicating not much of a street. I recognized Dundee Cottage, now called something else, and Villa Crepina, where the Crépin boys had lived. They threw stones at other people's dogs, especially English dogs. Their low evergreen hedge along the sidewalk still put out red berries. I had once been warned not to touch the leaves or berries, said to be poisonous. I ate only small quantities of leaves, and nothing happened. They tasted like strong tea, also forbidden, and desirable on that account. There was a fairy-tale look of danger about the berries. One could easily imagine long fairy-tale sleep.

At the cafe I spoke to some men sitting huddled at a counter. The place had gone silent when we came in speaking English. I asked if anyone had ever heard of families I remembered—the Duranseaus, whose children I had played with, or the tenants of Dundee Cottage, whose name suddenly returned and has again dissolved, or another elderly neighbour—elderly in recollection, perhaps not even forty—who complained to my mother when I said "bugger" and complained again when I addressed him, quite cheerfully, as "old cock." I had no idea what any of it meant. None of the men at the counter looked my way. Their hunched backs spoke the language of small-town distrust. Finally, a younger man said he was a relation of the Crépins. He must have been born a whole generation after the time when I picked a poisoned leaf whenever I went by his great-uncle's hedge. He knew about our house, so radically modified now, because of some child, a girl, who had lived there a long time before and been drowned in the river. He gave me his great-aunt's telephone number, saying she knew about every house and stone and tree and vanished person. I never called. There was nothing to ask. Another English-Canadian family with just one child had lived on the same side of the river. They had a much larger house, with a stone wall around it, and the drowned child was a boy. The Protestant school was named after him.

The fear that I had inherited a flawed legacy, a vocation without the competence to sustain it, haunted me from early youth. It was the reason why I tore up more than I saved, why I was slow to show my work except to one or two friends—and then not often. When I was twenty-one, someone to whom I had given two stories, just to read, handed them to a local literary review, and I was able to see what a story looked like surrounded by poetry and other fiction. I sent another story to a radio station. They paid me something and read it over the air, and I discovered what my own work could sound like in a different voice. After that I went on writing, without attempting to have anything published or asking for an opinion, for another six years. By then I was twenty-seven and becoming exactly what I did not want to be: a journalist who wrote fiction along some margin of spare time. I thought the question of writing or stopping altogether had to be decided before thirty. The only solution seemed to be a clean break and a try: I would give it two years. What I was to live on during the two years does not seem to have troubled me. Looking back, I think my entire concentration was fixed on setting off. No city in the world drew me as strongly as Paris. (When I am asked why, I am unable to say.) It was a place where I had no friends, no connections, no possibility of finding employment should it be necessary—although, as I reasoned things, if I was to go there with a job and salary in mind, I might as well stay where I was— and where I might run out of money. That I might not survive at all, that I might have to be rescued from deep water and ignominiously shipped home, never entered my head. I believed that if I was to call myself a writer, I should live on writing. If I could not live on it even simply, I should destroy every scrap, every trace, every notebook, and live some other way. Whatever happened, I would not enter my thirties as a journalist—or an anything else— with stories piling up in a picnic hamper. I decided to send three of my stories to *The New Yorker,* one after the other. One acceptance would be good enough. If all three were refused, I would take it as decisive. But then I did something that seems contradictory and odd: A few days before I put the first story in the mail (I was having all the trouble in the world measuring if it was all right or rubbish), I told the newspaper's managing editor I intended to quit. I think I was afraid of having a failure of nerve. Not long before, the newspaper had started a pension plan, and I had asked if I could keep out of it. I had worked in an office where I had watched people shuffle along to retirement time, and the sight had scared me. The managing editor thought I was dissatisfied about something. He sent me to someone else, who was supposed to find out what it was. In the second office, I was told I was out of my mind; it was no use training women, they always leave; one day I would come creeping back, begging for my old job; all reporters think they can write; I had the audacity to call myself a writer when I was like an architect who had never designed a house. I went back to my desk, typed a formal resignation, signed it, and turned it in.

The first story came back from *The New Yorker* with a friendly letter that said, "Do you have anything else you could show us?" The second story was taken. The third I didn't like anymore. I tore it up and sent the last of the three from Paris.

Newspaper work was my apprenticeship. I never saw it as a drag or a bind or a waste of time. I had no experience and would never have been taken on if there had been a man available. It was still very much a man's profession. I overheard an editor say, "If it hadn't been for the goddamned war, we wouldn't have hired even one of the goddamned women." The appalling labour laws of Quebec made it easy for newspapers to ban unions. I received half the salary paid to men and I had to hear, frequently and not only from men, that I had "a good job, for a girl." Apparently, by holding on to it I was standing in the way of any number of qualified men, each with a wife and three children to support. That was the accepted view of any young female journalist, unless she was writing about hem lines or three-fruit jam.

My method of getting something on paper was the same as for the fiction I wrote at home: I could not move on to the second sentence until the first sounded true. True to what? Some arrangement in my head, I suppose. I wrote by hand, in pencil, made multitudinous changes, erased, filled in, typed a clean page, corrected, typed. An advantage to early practice of journalism is said to be that it teaches one how to write fast. Whatever I acquired did not include a measure of speed. I was always on the edge of a deadline, and even on the wrong side. Thinking back on my outrageous slowness, I don't know why I wasn't fired a dozen times. Or, rather, perhaps I do: I could write intelligible English, I was cheaper by half than a man, and I seemed to have an unending supply of ideas for feature stories and interviews, or picture stories to work on with a photographer. It was the era of photo features. I liked inventing them. They were something like miniature scripts; I always saw the pictures as stills from a film. I knew Quebec to the core, and not just the English-speaking enclaves of Montreal. I could interview French Canadians without dragging them into English, a terrain of wariness and ill will. I suggested stories on subjects I wanted to know more about and places I wanted to see and people I was curious to meet. Only a few were turned down, usually because they scraped against political power or the sensibilities of advertisers. I wrote feature stories from the beginning; was an occasional critic, until I gave a film an impertinent review and a string of theatres cancelled a number of ads; wrote a weekly column, until the head of an agency protested about a short item that poked fun at a radio commercial, at which point the column was dropped. All this is a minor part of the social history of an era, in a region of North America at a political stand-still.

I managed to carve out an astonishing amount of autonomy, saved myself from writing on the sappy subjects usually reserved for women, and was not sacked—not even when someone wrote to protest about "that Marxist *enfant terrible.*" (It was not a safe time or place for such accusations.) My salary was modest, but whole families were living on less. I had amassed an enormous mental catalogue of places and people, information that still seeps into my stories. Journalism was a life I liked, but not the one I wanted. An American friend has told me that when we were fifteen I said I intended to write and live in Paris. I have no recollection of the conversation, but she is not one to invent anecdotes based on hindsight. It is about all I have in the way of a blueprint. The rest is memory and undisputed evidence.

The impulse to write and the stubbornness needed to keep going are supposed to come out of some drastic shaking up, early in life. There is even a term for it: the shock of change. Probably, it means a jolt that unbolts the door between perception and imagination and leaves it ajar for life, or that fuses memory and language and waking dreams. Some writers may just simply come into the world with overlapping vision of things seen and things as they might be seen. All have a gift for holding their breath while going on breathing: It is the basic requirement. If shock and change account for the rest of it, millions of men and women, hit hard and steadily, would do nothing but write; in fact, most of them don't. No childhood is immunized against disturbance. A tremor occurs underfoot when a trusted adult says one thing and means another. It brings on the universal and unanswerable wail "It's not fair!"—to which the shabby rejoinder that life isn't does nothing to restore order.

I took it for granted that life was tough for children and adults had a good time. My parents enjoyed themselves, or seemed to. I wish to bring back a Saturday night in full summer, couples dancing on the front gallery (Quebec English for veranda), a wind-up gramophone and a stack of brittle records, all I need to hear is the beginning of "West End Blues." The dancers are down from Montreal or up from the States, where there is Prohibition. Prohibition would be out of the question in Quebec, although the rest of Canada enjoys being rather dry. I mention it just to say that there is no such thing as a Canadian childhood. One's beginnings are regional. Mine are wholly Quebec, English and Protestant, yes, but with a current of French and Catholic. My young parents sent me off on that current by placing me in a French convent school, for reasons never made plain. I remember my grandmother's saying, "Well, I give up." It was a singular thing to do and in those days unheard of. It left me with two systems of behaviour, divided by syntax and tradition: two environments to consider, one becalmed in a long twilight of nineteenth-century religiosity; two codes of social behaviour; much practical experience of the difference between a rule and a moral point.

Somewhere in this duality may be the exact point of the beginning of writing. All I am certain of is that the fragile root, the tentative yes or no was made safe by reading. I cannot recall a time when I couldn't read; I do remember being read to and wanting to take the book and decipher it for myself. A friend of my parents recalled seeing my father trying to teach me the alphabet as I sat in a high chair. He held the book flat on a tray—any book, perhaps a novel, pulled off a shelf—and pointed out the capital letters. At a young age, apparently, I could translate at sight, English to French, reading aloud without stumbling. I was in no other way precocious: For years I would trail far behind other children in grasping simple sums or telling the time (I read the needles in reverse, five o'clock for seven) or separating left from right. I thought the eldest child in a family had been born last. At seven, I wondered why no one ever married some amiable dog. When my mother explained, I remained unenlightened. (The question possibly arose from my devoted reading of an English comic strip for children, *Pip and Squeak*, in which a dog and a penguin seemed to be the parents of a rabbit named Wilfred.) I did not know there was a particular bodily difference between boys and girls until I was eight; I had thought it a matter of clothes, haircuts, and general temperament. At nine, I still looked for mermaids in the Chateauguay River. My father had painted for me a screen that showed mermaids, with long red hair, rising out of green waves. I had not yet seen an ocean, just lakes and rivers. The river across the road froze white in winter and thawed to a shade of clear golden brown. Apart from the error as to colour, it seemed unlikely he would paint something untrue.

    Four weeks after my fourth birthday, when I was enrolled as a boarder in my first school, run by a semi-cloistered order of teaching and missionary nuns, I brought, along with my new, strange, stiff, uncomfortable and un-English uniform and severely buttoned underclothes, some English storybooks from home. (I owned a few books in French, the gift of a doctor, a French-Canadian specialist, who had attended me for a mastoid infection after scarlet fever and become a close friend of my parents. I was far too young to understand them. They were moral tales for older children, and even years later I would find them heavy going.) It was a good thing—to have books in English, that is—because I would hear and speak next to no English now, except in the summer holidays and at Christmas and Easter and on the odd weekend when I was fetched home. I always went back to school with new books, which had to be vetted: but no one knew any English and the nun who taught it could not speak it at all, and so the illustrations were scanned for decency and the books handed back to be stored in the small night-table next to my bed.

I owe it to children's books—picture books, storybooks, then English and American classics—that I absorbed once and for all the rhythm of English prose, the order of words in an English sentence and how they are spelled. I was eight before I was taught to write and spell English in any normal way, and what I was taught I already knew. By then, English was irremovably entrenched as the language of imagination. Nothing supposed, daydreamed, created, or invented would enter my mind by way of French. In the paper-doll era, I made up a mishmash of English, French, and the mysterious Italian syllables in recordings of bel canto, which my mother liked and often played. I called this mixture "talking Marigold." Marigold faded soon, along with paper dolls. After that, for stories and story-telling there was only one sound.

The first flash of fiction arrives without words. It consists of a fixed image, like a slide or (closer still) a freeze frame, showing characters in a simple situation. For example, Barbara, Alex, and their three children, seen getting down from a train in the south of France, announced "The Remission." The scene does not appear in the story but remains like an old snapshot or a picture in a newspaper, with a caption giving all the names. The quick arrival and departure of the silent image can be likened to the first moments of a play, before anything is said. The difference is that the characters in the frame are not seen, but envisioned, and do not have to speak, be explained. Every character that comes into being with a name (which I may change), an age, a nationality, a profession, a particular voice and accent, a family background, a personal history, a destination, qualities, secrets, an attitude towards love, ambition, money, religion, and a private centre of gravity.

Over the next several days I take down long passages of dialogue. Whole scenes then follow, complete in themselves but like disconnected parts of a film. I do not deliberately invent any of this: It occurs. Some writers say they actually hear the words, but I think "hear" is meant to be in quotation marks. I do not hear anything: I know what is being said. Finally (I am describing a long and complex process as simply as I can), the story will seem to be entire, in the sense that nearly everything needed has been written. It is entire but unreadable. Nothing fits. A close analogy would be an unedited film. The first frame may have dissolved into sound and motion (Sylvie and her mother, walking arm in arm, in "Across the Bridge") or turn out to be the end (Jack and Netta in Place Masséna, in "The Moslem Wife") or something incidental, such as the young Angelo begging for coins from Walter, which barely figures in "An Unmarried Man's Summer."

Sometimes one sees immediately what needs to be done, which does not mean it can be done in a hurry: I have put aside elements of a story for months and even years. It is finished when it seems to tally with a plan I surely must have had in mind but cannot describe, or when I come to the conclusion that it cannot be written satisfactorily any other way; at least, not by me. A few times, the slow transformation from image to fiction has begun with something actually glimpsed: a young woman reading an airmail letter in the Paris Metro, early in the morning; a man in Berlin eating a plate of cold cuts, next to a lace curtain that filters grey afternoon light; an American mother, in Venice, struggling to show she is having a fine time, and her two tactful, attentive adolescent children. Sometimes, hardly ever, I have seen clearly that a character sent from nowhere is standing in for someone I once knew, disguised as thoroughly as a stranger in a dream. I have always let it stand. Everything I start glides into print, in time, and becomes like a house once lived in.

There is something I keep wanting to say about reading short stories. I am doing it now, because I may never have another occasion. Stories are not chapters of novels. They should not be read one after another, as if they were meant to follow along. Read one. Shut the book. Read something else. Come back later. Stories can wait.

LITERATURE

SHARON BUTALA,

"Telling the Truth"

"Telling the Truth" engages not only the writing of stories but also the condition and situation of women writers in a patriarchal society. Whereas McCormack emphasizes "making it up," Butala stresses "being true to oneself (to herself)." She is very insistent regarding her position that drawing on her life as a woman doesn't diminish her achievement as a writer of fiction. She is not, she asserts, an autobiographer. Yet Butala emphasizes that her experiences as a woman are compelling and important enough to be shaped into fiction. That it is painful to produce such art Butala makes abundantly clear. Her essay is far more forceful than are the pieces produced by McCormack and Gallant; that is not necessarily to say that hers is better than theirs.

Questions:

1. Butala claims that women's short stories should be different than men's. Discuss.
2. What, for Butala, is the "Creative Flow"?
3. How can one be honest in fiction writing—something the author insists is vital?
4. Feminist fiction and feminist literary criticism have had a great impact on the world of literature. Discuss.
5. Is Butala too hard on "liars"?

Early on in my career as a writer, in the middle of an interview when the reporter had asked me a searching question, I remember it occurring to me for the first time that I could lie—that is, obfuscate, refuse to be engaged in the question, offer a polite untruth in response that no one would ever know. I hesitated the briefest of seconds, then I decided to at least attempt the truth. It was a permanent decision, and one I have adhered to.

In fact, it was a renewal of a vow I made long ago, when I was twelve or thirteen years old and a timid, but imaginative, and I think, somewhat emotionally neglected child, attending what we used to say with pride was "the toughest school in the city" (which meant of course, the school where the poorest kids went). I was caught in a lie by one of my friends, I had said I had seen certain kids in a certain place the night before, and my friend declared triumphantly that she had, at the same time, seen them somewhere else. Because our teacher was out of the room, as he often was, and anarchy reigned, this happened in front of the entire class. (Our teacher would return suddenly to use his fists on one of the boys or to be sexually improper in a subtle way with one of us girls.)

Being caught so publicly in a lie was a bitter experience for me. Despite the triviality of the issue, and while it stood out in my life for years as the greatest humiliation anyone could suffer, I was also immediately, grimly grateful for it, for I could see I was allowing myself more and more to be lured into that delightful world of the chronic liar, where whatever pops into one's head, one says, and life becomes playful and exciting instead of dull and ordinary—lying not out of malevolence, but out of impotence and steady disappointment.

I was no longer a liar, had been by a sudden, harsh measure turned into a fanatic truth-teller. It was a step towards my moral redemption, towards my becoming a member of the human race, to which till that moment, I had not belonged; the first moment when I began to be a person, not knowing till then how to be one and, sobbing by myself in that gloomy cloakroom, knowing I was being watched by my now repulsively sympathetic friends, I began that day, grounded in the imperative of truth-telling, the search for my self.

I had been brought up, as another ideal, to know that it was impolite, worse, vulgar, to talk about oneself, that the highest virtue (though I saw little of it around me) was self-effacement.

I did not aspire with any seriousness to such an ideal. I knew I couldn't keep quiet; I knew whenever I was self-effacing it was out of feelings of shame, guilt, embarrassment, inferiority, and not out of the serene knowledge of a higher way. Occasionally, over the years I tried silence, but wonderfully moral though it apparently was, biting my tongue never felt as profoundly satisfying as did speaking, and especially not as searching hard for and speaking what, as well as I could tell, was the truth.

While truth-telling seems more vital to me with every passing year (modified only by the consideration that in some instances one tells only as much truth as the other can bear), in time I came to see that moral ideal of silence about oneself as a useless ethic. It began to seem to be designed for those who had power, not for those who were powerless, designed for those with an abundance of self, not for those who had none. I began to suspect it to be self-aggrandizing, arrogant and hypocritical; I began, in fact, to see it as mere secrecy, used smugly most of the time to increase one's power by excluding others. And given that the style of our society, the ethical and moral values we accept, have been pretty much determined for us by male thinkers out of the male understanding of life, I see that desire, that need for secrecy as regrettably male.

"The personal is political," we are told, and I believe it. I think we women do not know who we are as a race, a species, a tribe. We have had no written history exclusively our own; when we have told our stories we have bent them to make them fit that version we are told by our culture is acceptable and true, left out the parts that didn't fit, kept silent out of the shaming belief that what is true for us as individuals is probably only a vile aberration; that is, we have lied. Often we haven't even told the truth to ourselves, because if we did, we would have to face our condition and that would be beyond the endurable, especially if we felt, and most of us do, that we cannot act to change it. (I mean by this everything from the abused wife who feels she cannot leave her husband, to the larger condition of all women, without exception, in a patriarchal society.) It is better not to look, most of us think; it is better not to acknowledge our true situation.

Not keeping silent about our lives, our experiences, and telling the truth about them—all the way down to the hardest, most humiliating, the most shameful parts—are the two things I believe we women are still not doing, and that I believe we must do before we can establish who we genuinely are as half the human race. As writers, it seems to me, we can do more than most towards discovering and delineating our history. We can do this by telling our true stories, the ones that will, at last, after centuries of suffering, help us recover our power as individual women, and as an equal part of creation.

It took me a long time to understand what a fiction writer does and how, and from there a long time to realize how important it is as a writer, a woman writer, to find the truth and tell it as compellingly as possible. I felt liberated the day or the week—it didn't happen overnight—that I discovered that I did not have to invent my stories in the way that children make up fantastic tales (or become chronic liars), but that I could use all the stuff of real life, that my work itself then gained in power, that I felt writing become holy when I moved into real life when I wrote, instead of out of it.

It turns out that the only truth I know without much doubt is the one that is the story of my life. I mean the emotional truths, the precise descriptions of my experience of womanhood. I do not mean by this the exact details, the locations, the statistics as such, or necessarily even the things that happened to me.

Despite this explanation or disclaimer, in my writing life this attempt has left me open to the suspicion that what I write is the true—whatever that might be—story of my life, that incidents that I tell and the reactions of my character, often called "I," are true incidents that actually happened to me, the writer. Further, that what I am writing must therefore be autobiography and beyond that, that by writing autobiography, I am doing something that is inferior, not quite fair, not quite art, not what a fiction writer is supposed to do, that I am in fact, "confessing," which is apparently inferior to actually inventing, which presumably is what other not "confessional" writers do. Or else, that other writers deal with the great ideas, while "confessional" writers never get beyond the kitchen sink.

I object vehemently to a discrimination which insists that high art must be thus and so; I object because of its elitism, its narrow-mindedness, its exclusivity which, coming from the school of feminism which says women experience the world differently than men, denies women writers like me—and I do not think I am all that unusual—a place in the contemporary literary canon.

In today's mail there is a brochure for a conference on violence against women. It lists and elaborates on the four categories of abuse. I am not surprised to find I have experiences that fit into three of the four categories. But I have never been slapped, kicked, or threatened with physical assault by a man (well, once at a teenage party by a drunk boy, who, thankfully, wasn't a lot bigger than I am, so that I shoved him hard against the wall and ran away, and as a student out on a date with a boy who wanted to have sex with me but wasn't quite willing to go as far as rape, who deliberately and precisely hurt me in wrestling with me—do these count, I ask myself?).

But I do not think of myself as an abused woman, nor would any but the most ardent feminist see me as such. My experience is ordinary. Reading this list, I know I don't know a woman my age who hasn't been subjected to any of the acts listed. Why is our literature not full of this awareness of what the lives of women are really like?

I think the answer is because the whole structure of our society is such that incidents like complete strangers, boys, yelling obscenities at us from a passing car as we walk alone down a street, we don't even tell anyone. We don't because: a) a part of us is ashamed, as if these boys somehow know the truth about us which we ourselves only know about through the dark undertow that runs through our society saying that women are unclean, disgusting, bad, and it runs so deep that even we believe it though we try hard not to; b) because what could anyone do anyway? c) who would care besides other women? d) because we are just thankful none of them got out of the car and hit us or raped us, and therefore it was too trivial to think about; and e) because that's how it is in our society for women and we all know it. These little incidents, which are woven so tightly into the fabric of our lives from the time we are very young, so that we hardly notice them as indefensible, these we rub out, erase, push away, leave out of our stories.

As it is in interviews, so it is also in writing fiction. If we women are struggling to find our way in the world, our own way and not the way of our fathers, brothers and husbands, our writers can help us to find that way, not by writing propaganda, diatribes, feminist rhetoric, but in our fiction by searching and writing what we know to be the truth about women's lives out of our own lives.

To quote May Sarton in her *Journal of a Solitude:*

> My own belief is that one regards oneself, if one is a serious writer, as an instrument for experiencing. Life—all of it—flows through this instrument and is distilled through it into works of art. How one lives as a private person is intimately bound into the work. And at some point I believe one has to stop holding back for fear of alienating some imaginary reader or real relative or friend, and come out with personal truth. If we are to understand the human condition, and if we are to accept ourselves in all the complexity, self-doubt, extravagance of feeling, guilt, joy, the slow freeing of the self to its full capacity for action and creation, both as human being and as artist, we have to know all we can about each other, and we have to be willing to go naked.

As one who believes women experience the world differently than men, it seems to me that we must think about the world differently; as writers, it follows then that we would not only tell different stories, but that we would tell them differently than in conventional ways, that we would perhaps invent a new short story form built wholly out of the texture of our daily lives as women. (I believe this is what Alice Munro has done, leaving the rest of us in her celestial dust. As a writer of short stories she inhabits that wholly feminine world all the time and what comes out on the page is unique.)

The searching is the hard part. Margaret Atwood talks about all writers "wrestling with their angel." As any Bible reader will know, the reference is to Jacob who says to the angel, "I will not let you go, unless you bless me." It seems, on the surface, an apt and rather beautiful metaphor, one that may well be true for most writers, but it is not true for me. I never see myself, when I am writing, in this confrontational and aggressive way. Instead, I see myself trying to be still enough and pure and quiet enough that I will become a hollow vessel through which "the angel"—which I conceive of as the Creative Flow—will speak. May Sarton puts it like this:

> To do this takes a curious combination of humility, excruciating honesty, and (there's the rub) a sense of destiny or of identity. One must believe that private dilemmas are, if deeply examined, universal, and so, if expressed, have a human value beyond the private, and one must also believe in the vehicle for expressing them, in the talent.

For a long time as readers we women accepted polite fictions; when we began to be publicly angry in the late sixties and early seventies, books like Marilyn French's *A Woman's Room* were published to acclaim. I always found that book too heavily onesided, that French asked too little of her women characters, painting them as profoundly oppressed, but not expecting them to act in any way themselves to end their oppression. I remember conversations with another feminist about this issue, how we spoke privately to each other, not daring to say out loud in a meeting that we found French's version of reality another lie, though one weighted in our favour.

Years later Germaine Greer reversed herself again, Gloria

Steinem said publicly she had in one important respect lived her life the wrong way, and Deirdre Bair, Simone de Beauvoir's biographer, showed her to be not the fiercely independent woman we had been told she was. The three of them left many of us who had tried to live by the example we believed they were setting feeling betrayed and very angry. I had once thought their courage and brilliance exemplary and by comparison I felt myself inferior, hopelessly confused, and worst of all, a coward whose existence continued to hold women back. I ought to have known, I told myself, that what they said about how they lived their lives couldn't have been wholly true, as if they lived in some different universe than I did, where there was no remorse, no conflict, no mistakes, no bitter sorrow, no longing for the things one felt one should renounce.

But the fact is, I didn't know, and, my head full of their rhetoric, I could only blame myself for my weakness in the compromises I made in order to have the things in life I couldn't seem to stop myself from wanting: a husband, children, a career, a nice home; or for the incredible difficulty which I often wasn't up to, of trying to attain them. I thank them for their insights, for their intellectual clarity, for their truth-telling as far as it went, and I suppose to blame them for the places where they failed to see the truth about their own lives is to blame them for being human.

The lesson remains the lesson of the consciousness-raising groups of those days—telling the truth about one's life, the only truth that can matter, that we must tell this truth, and this alone, in both our fiction and non-fiction for, as Doris Lessing has said, for a writer there is no difference. We women readers no longer want either unmitigated "victim" stories, or stories whose protagonists are paragons of brilliance and courage and whose lives are a triumphal progress. We want instead stories charting both the setbacks and the gains of private life, the humiliations and the exaltation, the confusion and the clarity, the weakness and the strength, but above all stories rich with the thick, dark blood of humanity, pulsing with the contradictions and beauty of real life.

Glossary of Useful Terms

Grammar handbooks, composition texts, style sheets: all of these contain various definitions of the many specialized words that crop up in the practice or teaching of essay writing. Nonetheless, the following terms, because they are referred to or deployed in this book, are drawn to your attention:

Allusion: "I'm as fast as Muhammad Ali." That reference to Ali, a person who lives outside your essay, is called an allusion.

Ambiguity: Ambiguity might be a useful tactic; then again, it might not. This "doubling" is an example of ambiguity. Statements that could mean two or more things, thereby confusing the reader, sometimes draw the attention of that reader's red pen (and the mark, "ambig.") on your page.

Analogy: "Writing essays is as difficult as making a soufflé." Trying to explain a difficult concept in terms of something less complex— this is what an analogy does.

Argument: An argument for our purposes is not what you get into with family, friends, lovers, et. al., but the major point you're making in your essay.

Classification (taxonomy): Cheetahs, wildebeests, giraffes, dogs: this is a group that can be classified as "animals." When one examines a system of classification, one is studying taxonomy.

Definition: In writing academic essays, assume your reader knows the dictionary definition of a word—unless you are interested in a rare word or a word's etymology or history.

Diction: Someone (Tom Wolfe, to be specific) said that no one uses the word "jejune" anymore. Prove him wrong! Throw in "exculpate" or "imbroglio," too, when the occasion arises. A dictionary will come in handy.

Digression: Should you wander away from your topic (say, by introducing the topic of "raves" at this point), you are digressing. This tactic sometimes works.

Exaggeration: The editors have given you the best collection of readings ever! That might be an exaggeration—another tactic that sometimes succeeds.

Figurative language (metaphor/simile): Describe something in terms of something else—e.g., "your shoulders are as tempting as sex crimes"—and you've produced a metaphor or simile, the latter if your comparison includes "like" or "as."

Gender-inclusive language: Instead of using "man" to mean men and women, try…"men" and "women" or "people" or…. Also, when "he" refers to everyone, try "he or she."

Grammar: Consult a grammar handbook when you're readying the final draft of your essay. The mistake that occurs most frequently in essays we receive: it's…when the writer means "its." It's = it is; "its" is a possessive (so are his and hers—they don't have apostrophes).

Irony: I often say, "jeez, I enjoy teaching." This could mean what it says…or it could mean, with the appropriate tone and facial gestures—"I'd rather be scuba diving." Irony lets you say two (opposing) things at once.

Myth: Myth sometimes means "falsehood" and other times a whole system of beliefs. The latter is the one usually encountered in literary studies.

Parallelism: "I like to box, to wrestle and the chance to appear on the Jerry Springer Show." "To box" and "to wrestle" are infinitives; the third item in the list above should be an infinitive as well. This would create a parallel structure.

Parentheses: (Sometimes you will want to put a few remarks in brackets or parentheses to subordinate them or simply to give them their own space.)

Parody: If you like to treat topics irreverently, making fun of your subject (the object of your ridicule), then parody is for you. Exaggeration, irony, understatement: these are some of the devices available for you to use in writing your parody.

Polemic: You are argumentative (occasionally truculent or abrasive) when you write in a polemical fashion. The opposite of a polemical paper would be a disinterested or impartial one.

Quotation: "Yes! I said, yes, yes, yes." That's the last line of James Joyce's *Ulysses*. Cite it—or something else—and your essay will gain the weight of someone else's words in addition to your own.

Redundancy: When you say something twice or more, sometimes it's for emphasis and sometimes it's…redundant—you've repeated yourself more or less (for no good reason).

Rhetoric: The skill with which someone presents an argument is that person's rhetoric. The term has come to mean other more complex things in postmodern vocabularies, but we'll leave it there.

Satire: "Dissing" someone in an elaborate literary or journalistic manner produces satire.

Style: Just as you've got a fashion style—punk, preppie, both or whatever—you've got a prose style as well. Getting to know it means becoming conscious of yourself as a writer.

Symbol: Not all telephone poles are meant to stand for penises; nonetheless, some things do occasionally represent other things in—and out of—literature.

Theme: Your essay, no doubt, has some general focus that is usually encapsulated in the title you've chosen. "The Theme of *Catcher in the Rye*"—the title of a possible essay—has as its theme the theme of *Catcher in the Rye*.

Tone: Sometimes, you're serious; at other times, you're playful, angry, mournful, teasing. The tone of your essay can also reflect various moods.

Understatement: You are thankful this Glossary has come to an end. Now, that's an understatement (actually, you're VERY thankful it's done with!).

AGMV Marquis

MEMBER OF SCABRINI MEDIA

Quebec, Canada
2002